Math Made Easy

4th Grade Workbook

10 Minutes A Day
Problem Solving

Authors
Sean McArdle and Darius McArdle

Consultant
Alison Tribley

10-minute challenge

Try to complete the exercises for each topic in 10 minutes or less. Note the time it takes you in the "Time taken" column below.

DK London
Editors Elizabeth Blakemore, Jolyon Goddard
US Editor Allison Singer
US Math Consultant Alison Tribley
Managing Editor Christine Stroyan
Managing Art Editor Anna Hall
Senior Production Editor Andy Hilliard
Senior Production Controller Jude Crozier
Jacket Design Development Manager Sophia MTT
Publisher Andrew Macintyre
Associate Publishing Director Liz Wheeler
Art Director Karen Self
Publishing Director Jonathan Metcalf

DK Delhi
Senior Editor Rupa Rao
Senior Art Editor Stuti Tiwari Bhatia
Editorial Team Nayan Keshan, Nishtha Kapil
Managing Editors Soma B. Chowdhury, Kingshuk Ghoshal
Managing Art Editors Ahlawat Gunjan, Govind Mittal
Senior DTP Designer Tarun Sharma
DTP Designers Anita Yadav, Rakesh Kumar, Harish Aggarwal
Senior Jacket Designer Suhita Dharamjit
Jackets Editorial Coordinator Priyanka Sharma

This American Edition, 2020
First American Edition, 2015
Published in the United States by DK Publishing
1450 Broadway, Suite 801, New York, NY 10018

Copyright © 2015, 2020 Dorling Kindersley Limited
DK, a Division of Penguin Random House Company
20 21 22 23 24 10 9 8 7 6 5 4 3 2 1
001–322721–May/2020

All rights reserved.
Without limiting the rights under the copyright reserved above, no part of this publication may be reproduced, stored in or introduced into a retrieval system, or transmitted, in any form, or by any means (electronic, mechanical, photocopying, recording, or otherwise), without the prior written permission of the copyright owner.
Published in Great Britain by Dorling Kindersley Limited

A catalog record for this book is available from the Library of Congress.
ISBN 978-0-7440-3144-7

DK books are available at special discounts when purchased in bulk for sales promotions, premiums, fund-raising, or educational use. For details, contact: DK Publishing Special Markets, 1450 Broadway, Suite 801, New York, NY 10018
SpecialSales@dk.com

Printed and bound in Canada

All images © Dorling Kindersley Limited
For further information see: www.dkimages.com

For the curious

www.dk.com

Contents   Time Taken

- **4** Fractions and Decimals 1
- **6** Fractions and Decimals 2
- **8** Fractions, Decimals, and Percentages 1
- **10** Fractions, Decimals, and Percentages 2
- **12** Percentage Problems 1
- **14** Percentage Problems 2
- **16** General Calculations 1
- **18** General Calculations 2
- **20** General Calculations 3
- **22** Conversion Problems 1

Time Filler:
In these boxes are some extra challenges to extend your skills. You can do them if you have some time left after finishing the questions. Or these can be stand-alone activities that you can do in 10 minutes.

24	Addition and Subtraction 1		46	Conversion Problems 2
26	Addition and Subtraction 2		48	Understanding Charts 1
28	Fractions, Decimals, and Percentages 3		50	Understanding Charts 2
30	Fractions and Decimals 3		52	Time Problems
32	Area Problems 1		54	Simple Formulas 1
34	Area Problems 2		56	Simple Formulas 2
36	Multiplication and Division 1		58	General Calculations 7
38	Multiplication and Division 2		60	Conversion Problems 3
40	General Calculations 4		62	Harder Problems 1
42	General Calculations 5		64	Harder Problems 2
44	General Calculations 6		66	Parents' Notes and Answers

Fractions and Decimals 1

Get ready to try out your skills working with fractions and decimals.

1) A driveway connecting an entrance gate and a garage was 0.35 mi long. After a landslide, 0.04 mi of the driveway was damaged and had to be fixed. What length was unaffected by the landslide?

2) Each time a kettle of water is boiled, 0.04 l of water is lost in the form of steam. If there was 0.67 l of water in the kettle to begin with, how much was left after the water had boiled?

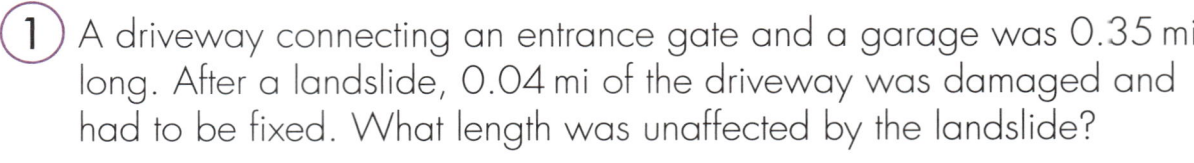

3) Jesse bought two bags of candy. One bag weighed 0.31 lb and the other weighed 0.78 lb. How much did the two bags of candy weigh together?

4) The gas tank of an average car has a capacity of 16 gallons. If you have filled half the tank already, how many more gallons of gas can the tank hold?

Time Filler:
Using a tape measure, measure in inches the length and width of a rectangular room in your home. Now convert each measurement into feet and inches.

5) Multiply these fractions and simplify the answer.

$\frac{3}{4} \times \frac{4}{5} = \boxed{} = \boxed{}$ 　　 $\frac{4}{3} \times \frac{2}{4} = \boxed{} = \boxed{}$

6) Calculate the following amounts.

$\frac{7}{8}$ of \$4 = ☐ 　　 0.6 of \$7 = ☐

7) Samir ate three-fifths of a pizza for lunch. In the evening, he felt hungry and ate one-half of the leftover pizza. What fraction of pizza did Samir eat altogether?

☐

8) Marilyn won \$50 in a painting competition and donated a quarter of her winnings to charity. How much money was Marilyn left with?

☐

Fractions and Decimals 2

How quickly can you solve these problems?
Some may be trickier than others!

1) John's school is five miles away from his home. On his way to school, John walks one mile and travels the rest of the distance by bus. What fraction of the journey does John walk daily?

2) At a department store, André spent half of his money on a shake and was left with $1.40. How much money did André start with?

3) The authorities plan to increase the length of an airport runway by 0.8 km. If it costs $1.23 million to lay 0.1 km of runway, how much will 0.8 km cost?

4) Dawn received $12 to spend on gifts. If she spent one-third of the money on her aunt's gift and the rest on her uncle's gift, how much money did Dawn spend on her uncle's gift?

Time Filler:
Write down these numbers: 12, 16, 20, and 24. Can you figure out what $\frac{1}{4}$, $\frac{1}{2}$, and $\frac{3}{4}$ of each number is?

5) Tim found out that two-thirds of a number is 16. What was the number?

6) What is half of each of these amounts?

$5 　　　3 miles 　　　11 pints

7) How much is half of $1.50? Write your answer in cents.

8) Brad spent two hours in a bookstore and a quarter of that time talking with a store assistant. How many minutes did Brad spend talking with the assistant?

Fractions, Decimals, and Percentages 1

Fractions, decimals, and percentages are closely related. Try to spot the connections between the three.

① Andrew spends 10% of his working day traveling between his two offices. If Andrew's usual working day is 8 hours, how long does he spend traveling between offices every day? Write your answer in minutes.

② In one season, a soccer team scored seven-twelfths of their goals in the second half. If the team scored 36 goals that season, how many of them were scored in the first half?

☐ goals

③ Cindy thought of a number and found out that 0.5 of that number is 14. What number did Cindy think of?

④ In a school, 50% of the students were boys. If there were 200 students in the school, how many of them were girls?

☐ students

Time Filler:
Write down your favorite subjects and then figure out what fraction of the school day you spend on each one. Now convert those fractions into decimals and percentages.

5) Out of 72 tourists traveling on a bus, 24 were from France. What fraction of the tourists was not from France? Simplify your answer as much as possible.

6) Danny participated in a charity run and covered 15 miles. He ran the first 12 miles and walked the last three. What fraction of the distance did Danny walk? Simplify your answer as much as possible.

7) When a crink is made from apples, three-tenths of the fruit is wasted. If 85 lb of apples is used, how much will be wasted?

8) A farmer grows corn on 6 acres of his land and potatoes on the other 12 acres of his land. On what fraction of the land does the farmer grow potatoes? Simplify your answer as much as possible.

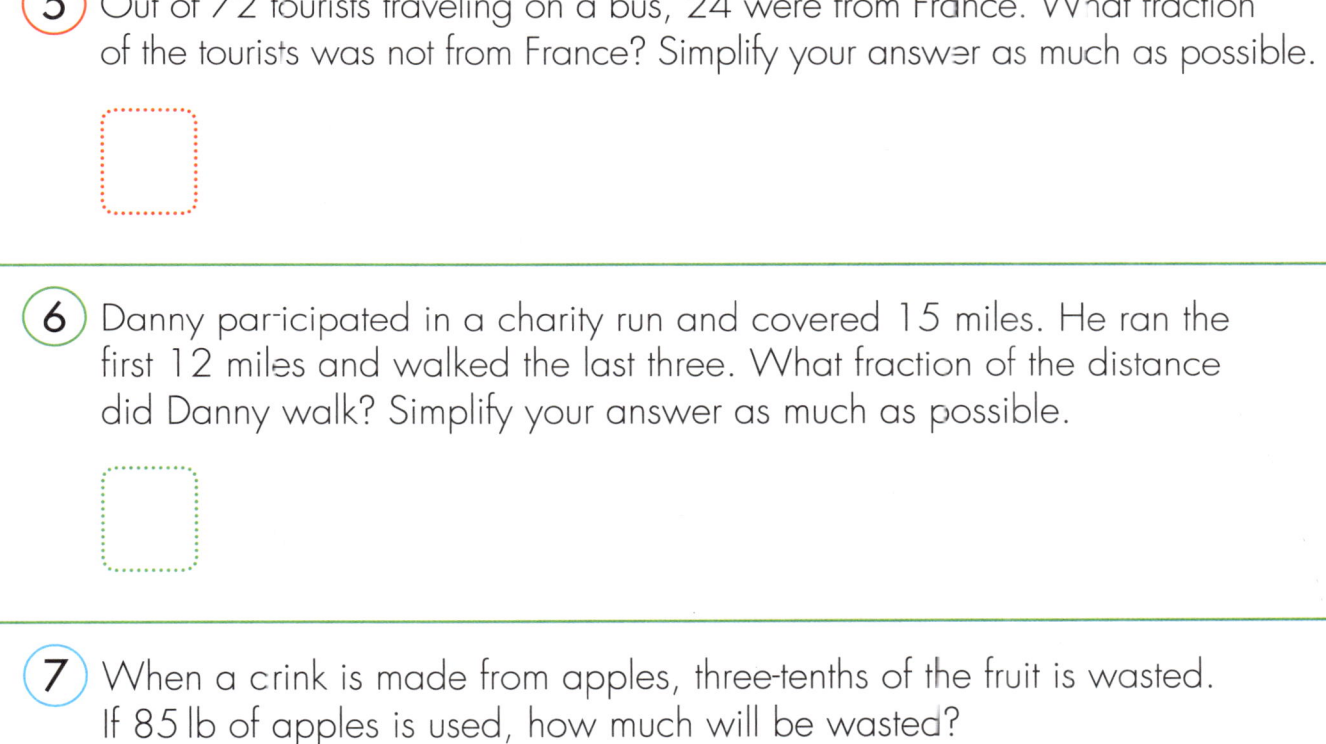

Fractions, Decimals, and Percentages 2

Get some more practice with these problems and see how quickly you can solve them.

1) Twenty percent of a garden is taken up by a patio. If the garden has a total area of 56 m², what is the area of the patio?

2) A bar of chocolate that usually costs 80¢ is on sale for 25% off. By how much money has the cost reduced?

3) Jenny received $12 from her father. She saved 0.8 of this money and spent the rest. How much money did Jenny spend?

4) Three-quarters of the audience at a music concert were below 18 years of age. If 600 people attended the concert, how many members of the audience were below 18?

people

Time Filler:
Using a ruler, measure the width of this page in centimeters. Now write your answer in meters using fractions, then again using decimals.

5) A car's gas tank holds 12 gallons of gas when full. If the indicator shows that only a quarter of the tank is full, how much gas is there in the tank?

6) A teacher completed grading five out of 60 tests. What fraction of tests is yet to be graded?

7) Owen bought stationery at a store. He gave a $5 bill to the cashier. If the bill amounted to 95% of $5, how much change did Owen receive?

8) Evie got 60% of her answers correct on a math test. If the test had 30 questions, how many answers did Evie get wrong?

answers

Percentage Problems 1

These problems are based only on percentages. Keep in mind everything you know about them.

(1) The normal price of a video game was $39.90, but Anne bought it at a 10% discount during a sale. She also bought two handheld controls at $15.80 each and paid for the items with four $20 bills. How much change did Anne receive?

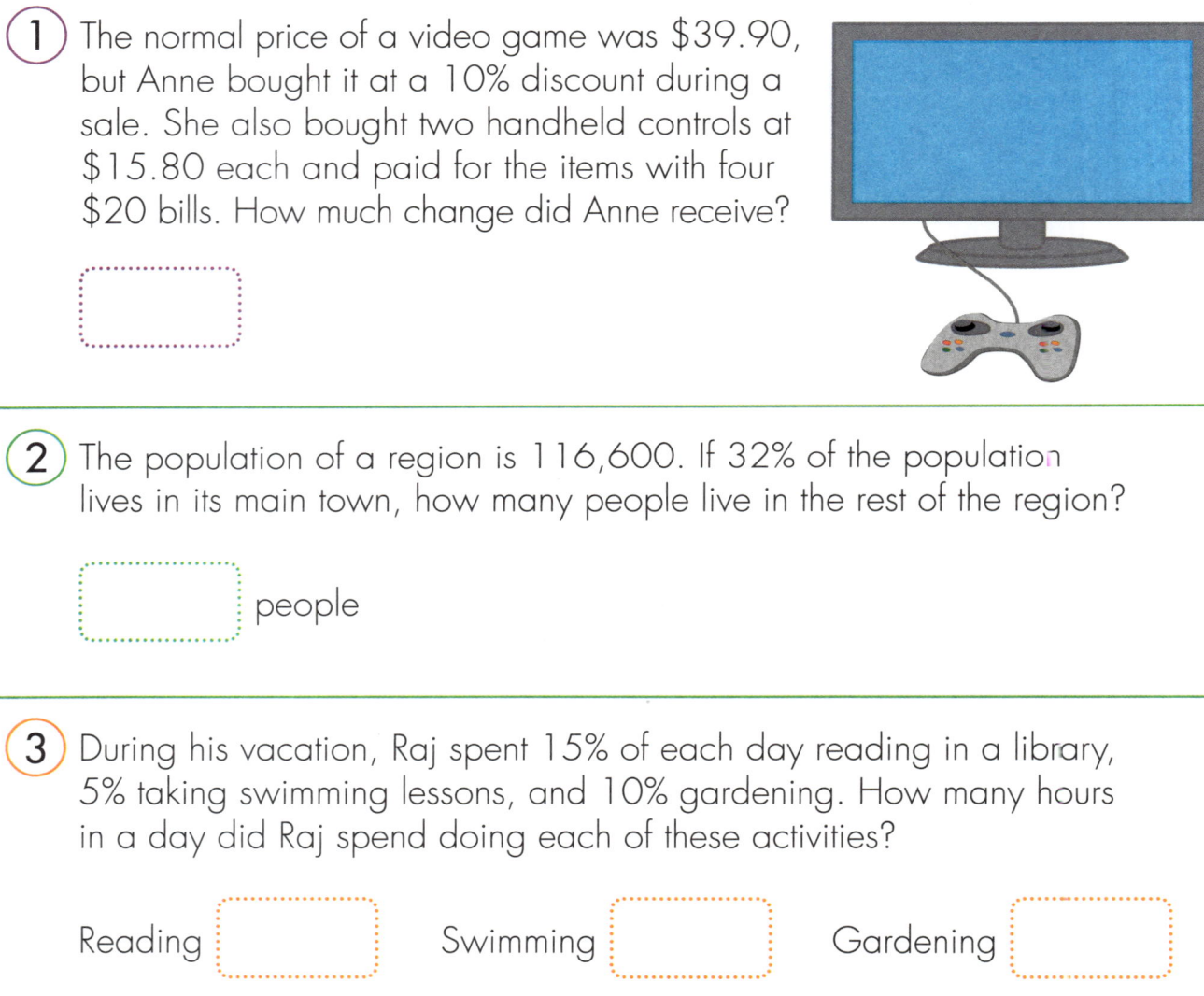

(2) The population of a region is 116,600. If 32% of the population lives in its main town, how many people live in the rest of the region?

⬚ people

(3) During his vacation, Raj spent 15% of each day reading in a library, 5% taking swimming lessons, and 10% gardening. How many hours in a day did Raj spend doing each of these activities?

Reading ⬚   Swimming ⬚   Gardening ⬚

(4) During a sale, Blayne bought a CD for $9. If he bought it at 25% discount, what was the original price for the CD?

⬚

Time Filler:
Find some oatmeal packets, soda bottles, or other packaged food items and see if they show the ingredients as percentages. Look carefully at the amount of sugar. Is it clearly labeled? If the percentage of sugar is shown, figure out how much sugar there is in the whole container.

5) Jack drove from Baltimore to Seattle, which is about 2,300 miles. He stopped for a break every 10% of the distance. After how many miles did Jack take his first break?

6) A television program lasted one hour but 10% of this time was taken up by advertisements. How long was the actual program?

7) As a birthday gift, Olivia received $20 from her grandparents. She spent 15% of it on music downloads, 20% on books, 25% on candy, and saved the rest. How much money did Olivia save?

8) Eighty percent of the cost of heating a house is spent October through April. If the cost of heating is $1,200 per year, how much money is spent during that period?

Percentage Problems 2

Solve these problems as quickly as you can.
Be sure to read the questions carefully.

1) A cargo of bananas weighs 2,000 kg. During transportation, 8% of the bananas rotted and cannot be sold.

What quantity of bananas cannot be sold?

Of the bananas that could be sold, 80% go to supermarkets and the rest to small stores. What quantity of bananas goes to the small stores?

2) In a school of 1,200 students, 40% study Spanish. Five percent of these students earn an A in Spanish. How many students earn an A in Spanish?

_____ students

3) Thirty children took a test and 10% of them got an A. How many children did not get an A?

_____ students

4) A doctor sees 15 patients in the morning and 10 in the afternoon. What percentage of the patients does he see in the morning?

Time Filler:
Have some fun with a million dollars! Write down what amount (and percentage) you would spend on each of the following: a house, cars, vacations, food, and clothes.

5) Sarah is given $25 in bills and coins. If bills make up 80% of the money, what is the value of the coins?

6) In a herd of cattle, 90% were Angus and the rest were Hereford. If the herd had 150 cattle, how many of each type were there?

Angus

Hereford

7) Elizabeth found out that 21 of her classmates preferred chocolate ice cream to any other flavor. If there were 28 children in Elizabeth's class, what percentage of children preferred chocolate?

8) A drama teacher had 40 children to help with a school play. Ten children were needed as actors and the others to help with the production. What percentage of children acted and what percentage worked as helpers?

Actors   Helpers

General Calculations 1

Read the problems carefully and make sure you understand exactly what you need to find out.

1) Emelia's dad gave her 5 ¢ on Sunday, double that amount on Monday, double that amount on Tuesday, and so on until Saturday.

How much money did Emelia receive on Saturday?

What was the total amount Emelia received from Sunday to Saturday?

2) Sean gave twice as much money to the Rescue a Rhino charity as he did to the Help a Hippo charity. If Sean gave $25 to Help a Hippo, how much money did he give to Rescue a Rhino?

3) A small township spends 20% of its money on education. If the township spends a total of one million dollars every year, how much money does it spend on education?

4) How many millimeters are the same as 2.45 m?

Time Filler:
Write a list of the first 15 square numbers. Make sure you can recognize them whenever you see them. You should also know instantly what number (square root) created the square number. For example, 3 is the square root of 9.

(5) Beth needs to stock up on food for a six-day camping trip. If Beth spends $12 on each day's food, how much money will she spend in total?

(6) Twelve out of every 1,000 dollar bills are damaged. What percentage of dollar bills is this?

(7) Jimmy normally receives $12 as allowance each week. The week before Christmas, he is given an extra 25%. How much will Jimmy be given in total that week?

(8) Mary has to divide a piece of material, which is 12 yards long, into six-inch strips. How many strips of equal length will Mary make?

_____ strips

General Calculations 2

How well can you answer these questions?
Try to be as accurate and quick as you can.

1) A class of children collected $80 for charity. They gave 30% to a pet charity and the rest to an African charity. How much did each charity receive?

Pet charity [ ]   African charity [ ]

2) A new series of books costs $15 per book. Allison bought five books in the series. How much did the books cost her in total?

[ ]

3) Mark covered 90 yards a minute, walking briskly. If he walked for 15 minutes, what distance did he cover?

[ ]

4) In a restaurant, a group of customers decided to pay a 15% tip. If the meal cost $80, how much will they leave as tip?

[ ]

Time Filler:
Did you know that a prime number is a number divisible only by 1 and itself. Write a list of the first 15 prime numbers.

5) The football field at a school was 360 feet long and 120 feet wide. If Angelo walked along the boundary of the field once, how far did he walk?

6) A mile is about 1.6 km. What distance is 26 miles in kilometers?

7) In a survey, 18 out of 50 people said they preferred cycling to walking. What percentage preferred walking?

8) Members of a movie club have to pay $7.50 every time they watch a movie. If six members of the club watched a movie once, how much did they pay in total?

General Calculations 3

Being able to solve problems like these is very important to developing confidence in math.

1. Daisy participated in a race. She ran one-tenth of the distance and cycled the rest. If the race was eight miles long, what distance did Daisy cycle?

2. A tennis court is 26 yards long. How long is the court in meters?
   Hint: a yard is about 0.91 m.

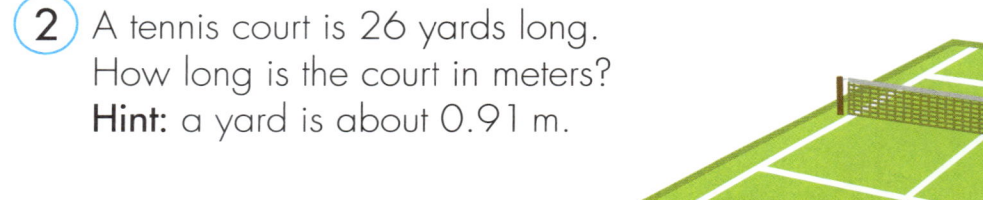

3. The price of a cell phone was $300. During a sale, the price was reduced by 25%. How much did the cell phone cost during the sale?

4. Convert 0.85 to a fraction and write the answer in its simplest form.

Time Filler:
Try some mental math: Begin with one and then double that to make two. Now double two to make four and so on. How far can you double and figure out the answer in your mind?

5) After a paintball match, only three players were left clean. If there were 24 players in all, what fraction was splattered with paint?

6) In a class of 30 children, 20 have pets. What fraction of children has pets? Simplify your answer as much as possible.

7) New tiles are being laid in a school corridor. Three-fifths of the area has already been tiled. If the total area to be tiled is 20 m², how much area is yet to be tiled?

8) A car journey from Kansas City to Harrisonville usually takes 40 minutes. During a traffic jam, the journey took 50% longer. How long did the complete journey take?

Conversion Problems 1

Learn all the conversions of the units that are frequently used. Soon, you will be able to recall them whenever required.

1 How many pounds are the same as 48 oz?

2 Brady bought four-and-a-half pounds of flour to bake a cake. How much flour is that in ounces?

3 If Mindy traveled eight miles by bus, how much did she travel in kilometers? **Hint:** a mile is about 1.6 km.

4 A carpenter needs to measure the length of a workbench in inches. If the workbench is 2 ft 8 in long, what is that length in inches?

Time Filler:
Give yourself some practice with converting some of the larger units. Find out the number of inches in a yard and the number of feet in a mile.

(5) Ron filled his tank with 25 gallons of gas. How much is that in pints?

(6) Emma cycles two miles to the park every evening and her brother Paul cycles one-and-a-half miles to the baseball field. How much farther does Emma cycle? Write the answer in yards.
Hint: 1 mile = 1,760 yards.

(7) Anne and her friends walked to school at a speed of 30 yards per minute. If they took 15 minutes to reach the school, how far did they walk?

(8) Martha collected pennies from the neighborhood to raise money for charity. If she collected 880 pennies in total, how much money did she raise? Write your answer as dollars and cents.

Addition and Subtraction 1

Always try to solve the problems in your mind as well as on paper.

1) A housing development project had 167 properties originally but an extra 68 were planned to be built later. How many properties were there after completion?

☐ properties

2) Mount Rushmore is 5,725 ft high. If a mountaineer has already climbed 3,650 ft, how many more feet remain to be climbed?

☐

3) Vincent received $150 for a present and Jules gave him another $95. How much money does Vincent have for the present altogether?

☐

4) Sonny calculated that he works 920 hours a month and his boss only works 540 hours a month. How many more hours does Sonny work than his boss?

☐ hours

Time Filler:
Write down three numbers that are less than 20. Examples are 19, 12, and 6. Now combine them by adding and subtracting in as many ways as you can. For example, 19 − 12 = 7 and 12 + 6 = 18.

---

5) The sum of two numbers is 500. If one of the numbers is 123, what is the other number?

---

6) Sandy collected 431 bubble-gum cards and Danny gave her another 106. How many cards does Sandy have in total?

_____ cards

---

7) Mary went on a road trip, which was 176 miles long. Her mother drove 89 miles and her father drove the rest. How many miles did her father drive?

---

8) Rick, Lisa, and Victor gave money to charity. Rick gave $23, Lisa gave $28, and Victor gave $21. How much money did they give altogether?

Addition and Subtraction 2

When you solve a problem, do the reverse calculation to check the answer. For example, 6 + 7 is 13 and 13 − 7 is 6.

1. Out of 496 peaches at a fruit mart, 164 were rotten and could not be sold. How many peaches could be sold?

   ☐ peaches

2. A small town had a population of 1,168 people. 1,096 people left the town after a drought. What was the population after the people left?

   ☐ people

3. When 250 is added to a number, the answer is 800. What was the original number?

   ☐

4. A number is twice the value of another number. If the two numbers are added together, the total is 36. What are the two numbers?

   ☐ and ☐

Time Filler:
Think of a small number such as 2 and keep doubling it mentally until you can go no further.

5) Will decreased a number by 58 and the new number was 76. What number did Will start with?

6) A town had 677 streetlights. As part of a development project, 42 new lights were put up. How many streetlights are there in total?

_____ streetlights

7) The total of three numbers is 1,000. If two of the numbers are 180 and 360, what is the third number?

8) Amy goes for a picnic to the countryside with her parents. The total distance is 68 miles. If they have already covered 43 miles, how much more distance do they still need to travel?

Fractions, Decimals, and Percentages 3

Can you solve all of these problems quickly?
Don't forget to check your answers.

1) Write each fraction as a decimal.

$\frac{9}{10}$ ☐ $\frac{7}{100}$ ☐ $\frac{2}{10}$ ☐

$\frac{1}{10}$ ☐ $\frac{4}{10}$ ☐ $\frac{4}{100}$ ☐

$\frac{5}{10}$ ☐ $\frac{11}{100}$ ☐ $\frac{21}{100}$ ☐

2) The cost of building a house is twice the cost of the land it is built on. If building a house costs $250,000, how much has the land cost?

☐

3) In a factory with 72 workers, one-sixth of the workers are male. How many workers are female?

☐ workers

4) Orange squash is a drink that is made by mixing one part concentrate to four parts water. At a party, four pints of concentrate are used. How many pints of water will be needed?

☐

Time Filler:
Simplify each of these fractions as much as you can:
$\frac{5}{20}, \frac{8}{40}, \frac{10}{100}, \frac{24}{72}, \frac{36}{144}$

5) What fraction of letters in the English alphabet are vowels? (Assume that the letter **y** is a consonant.)

☐

6) In a parking lot with 100 spaces, 35% of the spaces are reserved. How many spaces are open?

☐ parking spaces

7) In a box of chocolates, one-fourth of the candy was dark chocolate and the rest was milk chocolate. If there were 36 milk chocolates, how many dark chocolates were there?

☐ dark chocolates

8) Every time Ben plants three daisies, Pam plants one rose. If Pam planted 100 roses, how many daisies did Ben plant?

☐ daisies

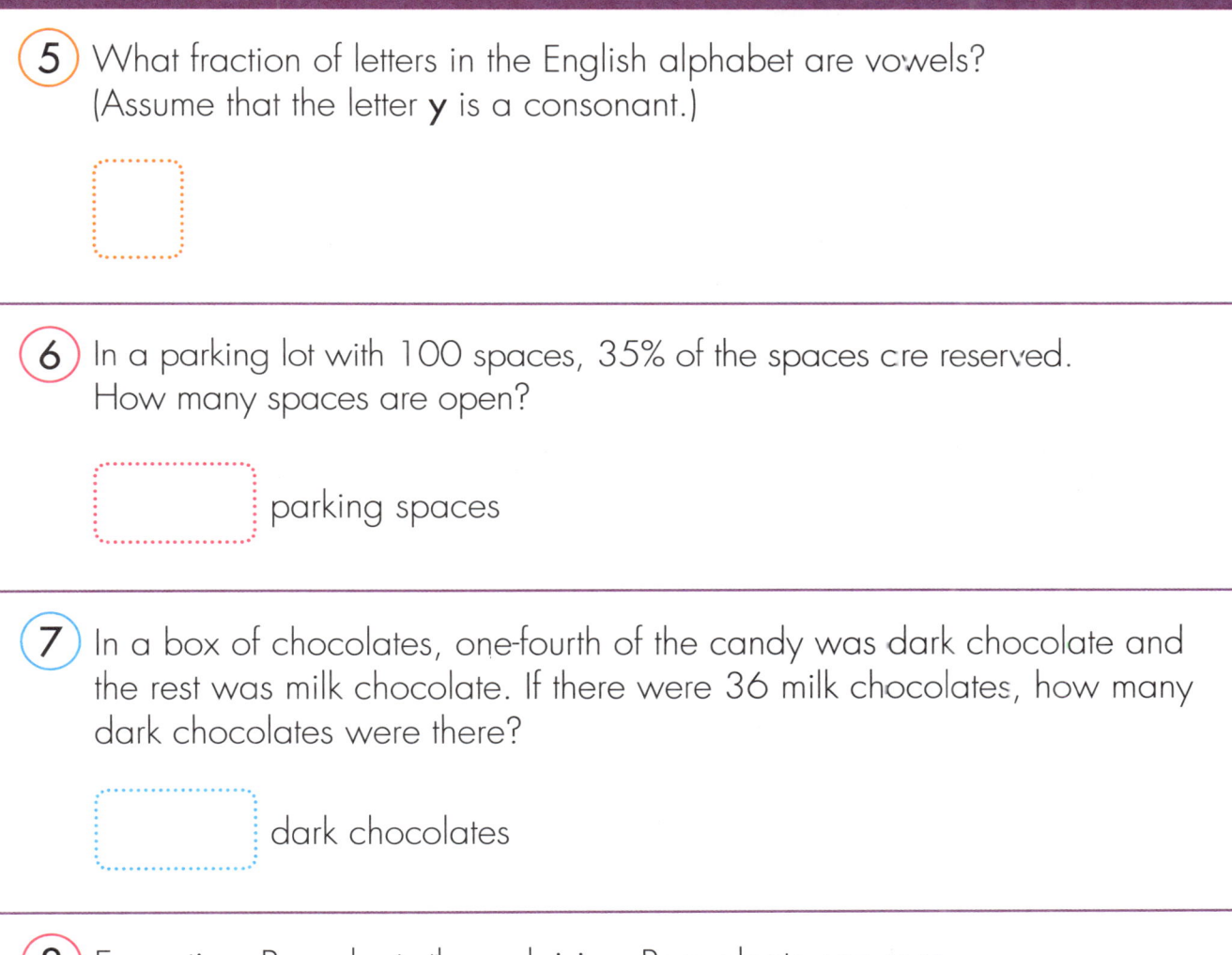

Fractions and Decimals 3

Here is some more practice with fractions and decimals. Get ready, go!

1. Write the fraction $\frac{100}{1,000}$ in its simplest form.

2. Write the fraction $\frac{60}{240}$ in its simplest form.

3. Forty-eight tennis players took part in a tournament. One-third of the players was left-handed. How many players were left-handed?

   ⬚ players

4. In a class of 30 children, one in five wears glasses. How many children wear glasses?

   ⬚ children

Time Filler:
Simplify these fractions as much as you can: $\frac{9}{24}$, $\frac{15}{100}$, $\frac{6}{54}$, $\frac{10}{1{,}000}$

5) The length of a rectangle is four times its width. If the length is 4.8 in, what is the width of the rectangle?

6) A farmer needs an acre of land for 10 cows. If he has 100 cows, how many acres of land will the farmer need?

_____ acres

7) On his trip to school, Bruce saw one-quarter as many trucks as he saw cars. If Bruce saw 96 cars on the way to school, how many trucks did he see?

_____ trucks

8) In the word "mathematics," what fraction of the letters are vowels?

Area Problems 1

Make sure you remember to write the correct units when working with area.

① A rectangle has an area of 18 in². The length of the rectangle is twice its width. Find the length and the width of the rectangle.

Length ☐   Width ☐

② A wall needs to be painted. It is 15 ft long and 9 ft high. Find the area that needs to be painted.

☐

③ A rectangle has an area of 9 yd² and two of its sides measure 4 yd. How much do the other sides measure?

④ A rectangle has an area of 100 ft². If the shorter sides measure 5 ft, how much do the longer sides measure?

Time Filler:
Roughly measure the sizes of each of the bedrooms in your house to the nearest foot. Then determine the area of each room. Which room has the biggest area and which the smallest?

(5) The width of a door is 4 ft. The height of the door is twice its width. Find the height and the area of the door.

Height ☐   Area ☐

(6) A rug was 5.5 yd long and 4 yd wide. Find the area of the rug.

(7) Two sides of a rectangular field were 8.5 yd and its area was 68 yd². How long were the other sides?

(8) A soccer field measures 105 yd by 68 yd. Find the area of the field.

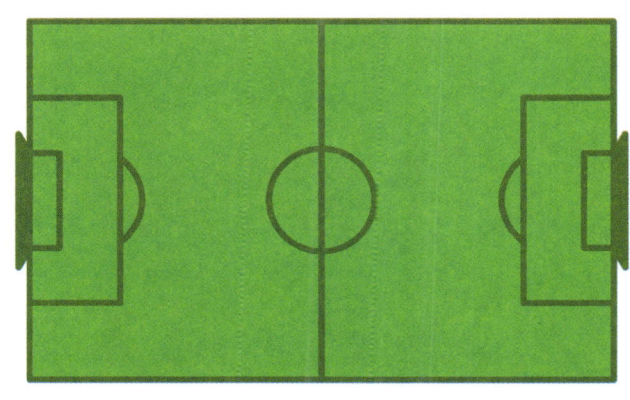

Area Problems 2

To solve these problems, you will need to know how to find the area of a rectangle.

① A sidewalk measures 30 yd by 3 yd. What is its area?

② A picture frame is a square with each side measuring 13 in. What is the area of the frame?

③ The area of a table top is 15 ft². What is half the area of the table top?

④ A square has an area of 225 in². What is the length of each side of the square?

Time Filler:
Estimate the area of the front cover of a few books and magazines. Then measure and solve for the areas accurately. How close were your estimates?

5) The screen of a TV installed outside a fast-food joint is 56 in wide and 30 in high. What is the area of the screen?

6) The height of a greeting card is twice its length. If the area of the card is 18 in², what are the lengths of the sides?

⬜ and ⬜

7) A laptop has a screen, which is 13 in wide and 9 in high. What is the area of the screen?

8) If a wall tile has an area of 24 in², what will be the area of 6 such tiles?

Multiplication and Division 1

So much of this work depends on plenty of times tables practice. Make sure to practice regularly.

① Every time Larry caught a frog in a computer game, he gained 15 points. If Larry catches 20 frogs, how many points will he have?

☐ points

② Alex scored three times as many points as the boy seated next to him on a math test. If the boy scored 35 points, how many points did Alex score?

☐ points

③ Lucy distributed 30 cookies equally among five of her friends. How many cookies did each friend receive?

☐ cookies

④ When Clark played a computer game, he gained 50 points every time he caught a bad guy. Clark had a good day and caught 12 bad guys. How many points did he score that day?

☐ points

Time Filler:
Write down any three numbers. For example, 2, 5, and 9. Now multiply them in as many combinations as you can think of. For example, 9 x 5 and 2 x 9 x 5.

5) The length of a rectangle is 1.5 cm and the width is 8 cm. Find its area.

6) Perry's birthday cake was cut into eight pieces and each piece had six chocolate candies on top. How many chocolate candies were there in total on the cake?

chocolate candies

7) Jimmy's parents give him allowance of 50 ¢ every week. If Jimmy has saved his money for 20 weeks to go on a vacction, how much money has he collected? Give your answer in dollars.

8) A teacher graded 30 tests each evening for five evenings. How many tests did the teacher grade in total?

tests

Multiplication and Division 2

Recall of times tables facts must not just be accurate but also as fast as possible.

① George multiplied a number by itself and got the answer 81. What number did George begin with?

② A driver collects five coupons every time he gets his gas tank refilled. If the driver refills 35 times in a year, how many coupons will he collect?

⬜ coupons

③ Billy divides a number by six and the result is 5 remainder 3. What number did Billy begin with?

④ A mailman delivers to 28 streets. Each street has 20 houses. How many houses does the mailman deliver to?

⬜ houses

Time Filler:
Write down 48, 60, and 64. Now write down all the numbers that divide exactly into each one.

5) A math teacher wrote 20 equations on the board and in the evening she checked the students' answers. If the teacher had to check 240 answers, how many children are in her class?

☐ children

6) Billy pays $15 every time he takes a swimming lesson. If Billy takes twelve lessons, how much will they cost him?

☐

7) A number multiplied by nine gives 180. What is the number?

☐

8) When a number is divided by five, the answer is 12 remainder 3. What is the number?

☐

General Calculations 4

Here are more problems for you to solve. They may seem tricky to start with but keep trying.

1) Stefan's father has to pay $114 for a train ticket to New York, but his grandfather pays 60% of that amount. How much less money does Stefan's father have to pay?

2) A waiter has calculated a customer's bill as $56. He then realizes he has added an extra meal and needs to reduce the bill by 25%. How much will the new bill be after the reduction?

3) When three different numbers are added together, their total is 47. One of the numbers is 20 and one of the other numbers is half the third number. What are the other two numbers?

☐ and ☐

4) If half of an amount is $26, what is the full amount?

Time Filler:
Find these amounts of 36:
$\frac{1}{2}$, $\frac{1}{3}$, $\frac{1}{6}$, $\frac{1}{12}$, $\frac{1}{9}$, 75%, and 100%.

5) When a number is multiplied by 12 and then halved, the result is 120. What is the original number?

6) Which three consecutive numbers add up to give a total of 90?
Hint: consecutive numbers are numbers that follow each other in order.

7) If the time now is 11:00 AM, what time will it be two hours later?

8) If it costs $150 to heat a house each month, how much will it cost for a whole year?

General Calculations 5

42

You will find a mixture of math topics in these questions. So, stay alert!

1) The average of two numbers is 7. If one of the numbers is 9, what is the other number?

2) A magazine costs $4.25 each month. Mona got an annual subscription, which cost her $48. How much money did Mona save over the year by subscribing to the magazine?

3) A squad of soccer players has 24 men. If a quarter of the players are goalkeepers, how many are not goalkeepers?

players

4) Which two prime numbers multiplied together give the product 91?

and

Time Filler:
Convert each of these decimals to a fraction in its simplest form: 0.85, 0.73, 0.34, and 0.02.

5) In a pile of 120 shirts, one-fifth are blue and three-tenths are white. How many shirts are neither blue nor white?

[ ] shirts

6) A cell phone screen is 5.5 in by 3 in. What is the area of the screen?

[ ]

7) A quarter of a number is 13. What is the whole number?

[ ]

8) A large bakery produces 3,600 cupcakes every day and has 24 workers to prepare them. How many cupcakes does each worker make in a day?

[ ] cupcakes

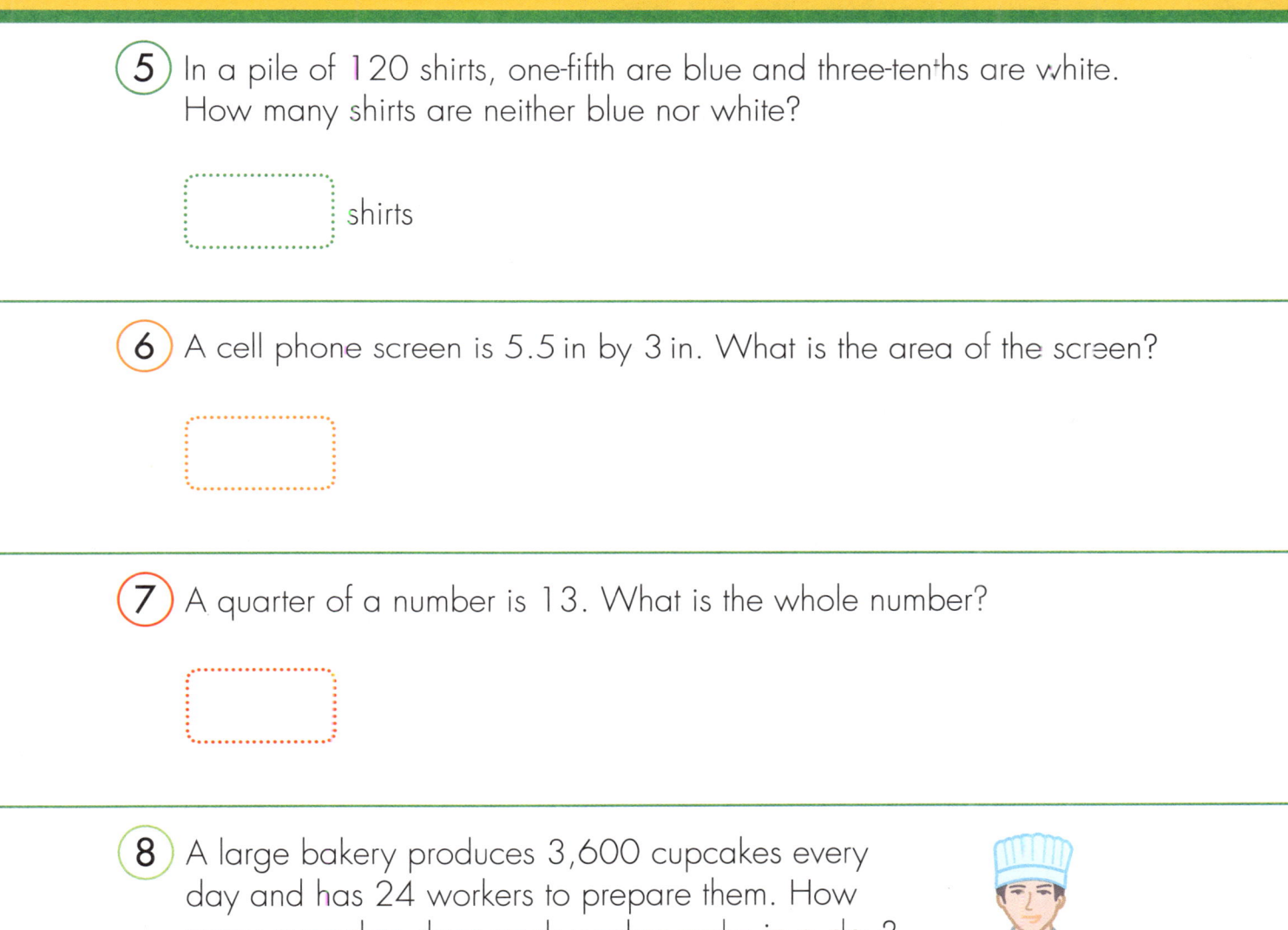

General Calculations 6

Always write down your calculations clearly so that you are sure of the numbers you have written.

① The brick foundation of a shed needs to be 4 yd long and 2.5 yd wide. If bricks cost $52 per square yard, how much will the foundation cost?

② Which shape has eight sides of equal length?

....

③ We can measure height in feet. If a child is 4.5 ft tall, how tall is the child in centimeters? **Hint:** a foot is 30.5 cm.

④ A builder tiled a bathroom floor and used twice as many white tiles as blue tiles. If the builder used a total of 36 tiles, how many of each color did she use?

White tiles

Blue tiles

Time Filler:
Write all the factors of these numbers and say which of these are prime numbers and which are squares:
16, 11, 80, 24, and 81.

⑤ A number when multiplied by itself gives 196. What is the number?

⑥ The cost of renting a chair at a beach is $1.50 an hour. If a family rents five chairs for six hours, what will be the total cost?

⑦ The area of a rectangle is 504 in². If the rectangle is 7 in wide, what is its length?

⑧ One angle of an isosceles triangle is 24° and the other two angles are equal to each other. What is the size of the other two angles?

Conversion Problems 2

You should be able to solve some of these in your head. Give them a try!

① A water tank holds 20 gallons of water. How much water is that in pints?

② A car's gas tank has a capacity of 16 gallons. If half of this quantity has been used up, how many pints are left in the tank?

③ Oliver's little sister is 3.5 ft tall. What is her height in inches?

④ A swimming pool is 15 yd long. How long is the pool in inches?

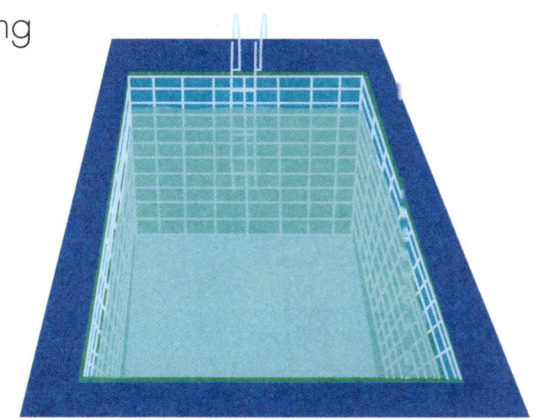

Time Filler:
Measure the lengths of some large objects, such as a table. Measure each one in inches. Now convert the measurements to feet and inches.

(5) A recipe requires the use of three pounds of flour. How much flour is needed in ounces?

(6) At a party, Jay served a pint of orange juice to each guest. If Jay served 96 pints of orange juice, how many gallons did he need?

(7) Daisy takes a walk and covers 400 yd in four minutes. How long will it take Daisy to walk 2,400 ft?

(8) If Scott has $3.75, how much money does he have in cents?

Understanding Charts 1

Understanding data in charts and tables can be very useful. You would never want to miss a bus or a movie!

Thirty children were asked to describe how they felt about school examinations. This pie chart shows their views.

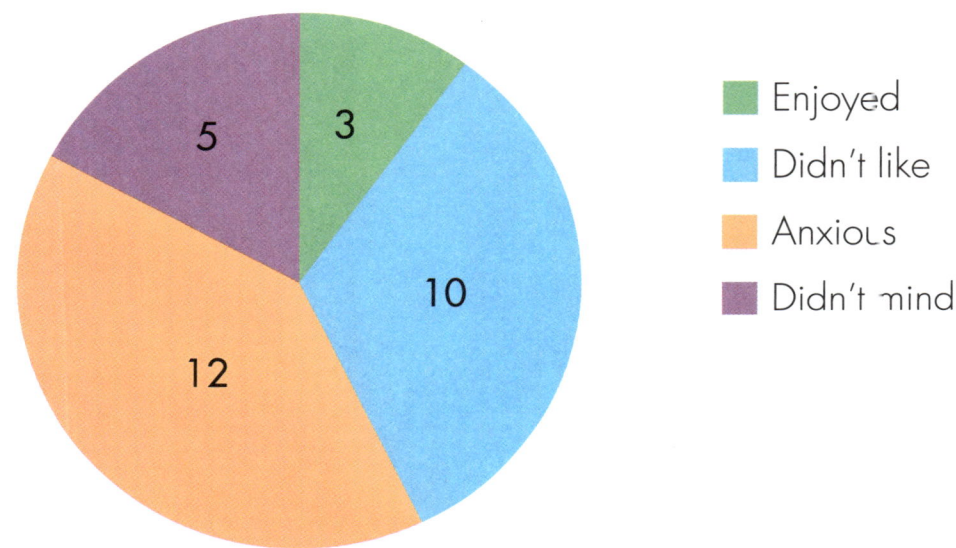

Children's Views on School Examinations

- Enjoyed
- Didn't like
- Anxious
- Didn't mind

1 What fraction of the children didn't mind taking exams?

2 Which was the largest group? ....

3 What percentage of the children enjoyed exams?

Time Filler:
Look in a newspaper or on the Internet to find a bus or a train timetable. How easy is it to find information? Is it clear or is it confusing?

④ How many more children didn't like exams than the ones who enjoyed them?

☐ children

⑤ What fraction of the total number of children were either anxious or didn't like the exams?

☐

⑥ Which group was two less than those who were anxious?

....

⑦ What was the average number of votes for each response?

☐ votes

⑧ If six children had said that they didn't mind taking exams, what fraction of the children would that be?

☐

Understanding Charts 2

Make sure you know what each column and row in a chart is showing you.

A teacher made a note of the number of children who ate fruit at lunchtime. These are her findings.

Day	Number of Children
Monday	15
Tuesday	26
Wednesday	20
Thursday	18
Friday	16

1. What is the average amount of fruit eaten each day?

2. How many more children ate fruit on Tuesday than on Monday?

    children

3. What fraction of the total amount of fruit was eaten on Monday?

4. Which day has the median number of fruit?
   Hint: median is the middle value in a series of numbers.

> **Time Filler:**
> Imagine you are going to find out information about your classmates. First, decide what you would like to investigate. Second, sort out the questions you will ask. Third, note the responses. Finally, decide on the best way to show your findings.

During the next week, each child was given free fruit every day and the teacher prepared a new chart.

Day	Number of Children This Week	Number of Children Last Week
Monday	36	15
Tuesday	51	26
Wednesday	40	20
Thursday	46	18
Friday	45	16

5) Which day had the largest increase in the number of children eating fruit?

....

6) Which day has the median number of fruit this week?

....

7) Which day has the smallest increase in the number of children eating fruit?

....

8) What is the average amount of fruit eaten each day this week?

Time Problems

You should learn simple multiples of 60 and 24, such as 5 x 60 and 8 x 24, to be able to convert between minutes and seconds, hours and minutes, and days and hours.

1. Walter went to school at 8:30 AM and returned home at 3:30 PM. How long has Walter been away from home?

2. A train journey takes 3 hours 48 minutes. If the journey begins at 10:45 AM, at what time will it finish?

3. Benjamin's helicopter ride started at 3:45 PM and ended at 6:00 PM. How long was the ride?

   ☐ hours ☐ minutes

4. A meal takes 35 minutes to cook in an oven. If the meal is put in at 4:53 PM, at what time will it be ready?

Time Filler:
Write down how long you spend each day watching TV, doing school work, playing computer games, and eating. Write the time in hours and minutes first and then in minutes.

5) A worker is paid by the hour. If he works eight hours a day for five days, how many hours does he work in five days?

6) It takes Barbara 15 minutes to get out of bed and eat her breakfast, twice as long as that to take a shower and get ready for school, and 25 minutes to walk to school. Barbara has to be at school by 8:30 AM.

For what time should Barbara set her morning alarm?

7) Write the time 30 minutes before each of these times.

   8:45 AM   2:20 PM   12:05 PM

8) Tyrone needs to write 200 minutes as hours and minutes. How many hours and minutes will that be?

   ☐ hours ☐ minutes

Simple Formulas 1

Keep in mind the formulas and times tables you have learned. They will help you solve these questions.

The area (A) of a rectangle is calculated by multiplying its length (l) by its width (w). The formula is written as $A = l \times w$ or $A = lw$.

① If the length of a rectangle is 8 in and the width is 4.5 in, find the area of the rectangle.

② If the length of a pencil box is 21 in and its area is 157.5 in², what is its width?

③ If the area of a book is 630 in² and its width is 21 in, what is its length?

④ If the length of a notebook is 12 in and the width is 11 in, find the area of the notebook.

Time Filler:
If the length of each side of the following shapes is 6 in, find their perimeters: equilateral triangle, square, pentagon, hexagon, octagon, and decagon.

The waist measurement (**W**) of an average man is half his height (**h**). The formula is written $W = \frac{h}{2}$. For the following questions, assume each person's measurements follow this formula.

5) If Jake's father is 6 ft 2 in tall, how much does his father's waist measure?

6) Mark's waist measures 26 in. Find out his height.

7) Noah's cousin is 72 in tall. What will his waist measurement be? Write your answer in feet.

8) Cary measured her grandfather's waist and it measured 37 in. How tall is her grandfather in feet and inches?

Simple Formulas 2

These questions introduce you to a part of math called algebra.

1) $a = b + c$ means **a** is the sum of **b** and **c**.

   If **a** is 19 and **c** is 7, find the value of **b**. ☐

   If **c** is 18 and **a** is 42, find the value of **b**. ☐

   If **b** is 29 and **a** is 58, find the value of **c**. ☐

2) $a = b \times c$ means **a** is the product of **b** multiplied by **c**.

   If **b** is 3.5 and **c** is 8, find the value of **a**.

   ☐

   If **a** is 70 and **b** is 14, find the value of **c**.

   ☐

   If **a** is 12, give three different pairs of whole numbers that could be the values of **b** and **c**.

   ☐   ☐   ☐

Time Filler:
If the area of a rectangle is 60 in², determine the different lengths of the sides the rectangle could have.

③ If a = b − c and a is 10, write three different pairs of numbers that b and c could be.

④ If a = $\frac{b}{c}$ and the value of a is 4, write three pairs of numbers that could be the values of b and c.

⑤ If a = 3b and b is 4, what is a? **Hint:** 3b means 3 × b.

⑥ If a = 3b and a is 21, what is b?

⑦ If a = 2b + 4 and the value of a is 16, what is b?

⑧ a = 2b + 4 means a is equal to twice b plus 4. If b is 6, what is a?

General Calculations 7

You should have become an expert by now. So concentrate on being quick and accurate!

1) A packet contains six greetings cards and costs $4.68. What is the average cost of each card?

2) Dan added three consecutive numbers and his total came to 45. Which numbers did he add?

3) Add the number of sides of an octagon to the number of sides of a decagon. Then divide the total by the number of sides of a triangle and write the answer.

4) Jake and his dad covered a total distance of 130 miles in 2 hours. At what speed did his dad drive the car?

Time Filler:
Write down two problems each for multiplication, division, subtraction, and addition that all give you the answer 8.

5) What amount is halfway between $70 and $100?

6) Martin spends $55 a month on food and Danny spends twice as much. How much money does Danny spend?

7) If a square has an area of 144 in², what is the length of each side?

8) On an average, a cow gives 1,600 gallons of milk each year. If a herd has 60 cows, how much milk will the herd give in one year?

Conversion Problems 3

Try your best to solve these problems involving conversion.

1) Harry's school is 3.5 miles away from his home. His karate academy is 1.8 miles farther away from his school. How far is the karate academy from Harry's home? Write your answer in yards.

2) A bag of apples weighs 4 lb and a bag of oranges weighs 56 oz. Which bag is heavier?

3) Amanda went on vacation to England with her family. She spent £300 there. How many dollars did she spend? **Hint:** a pound is worth about 1.69 US dollars.

4) The length of an undersea cable is 257,500 m. How long is the cable in kilometers?

Time Filler:
Test yourself and make sure you can convert weeks to months, months to years, and years to decades and centuries.

(5) Zara spends six hours in class at school every day and has a 40-minute lunch break in the cafeteria. How much time does she spend at school each day in total? Write your answer in minutes.

(6) A car travels at a speed of 60 mph. How far will it travel in 2 hours 30 minutes?

(7) The distance between Fargo, ND, and Phoenix, AZ, is 1,671 miles. How far is this distance in kilometers? Write your answer to two decimal places. **Hint:** one kilometer is 0.62 miles.

(8) Allie's pencil is 18.6 cm long, whereas Nancy's is 175 mm long. Whose pencil is longer and by how much? Write your answer in centimeters.

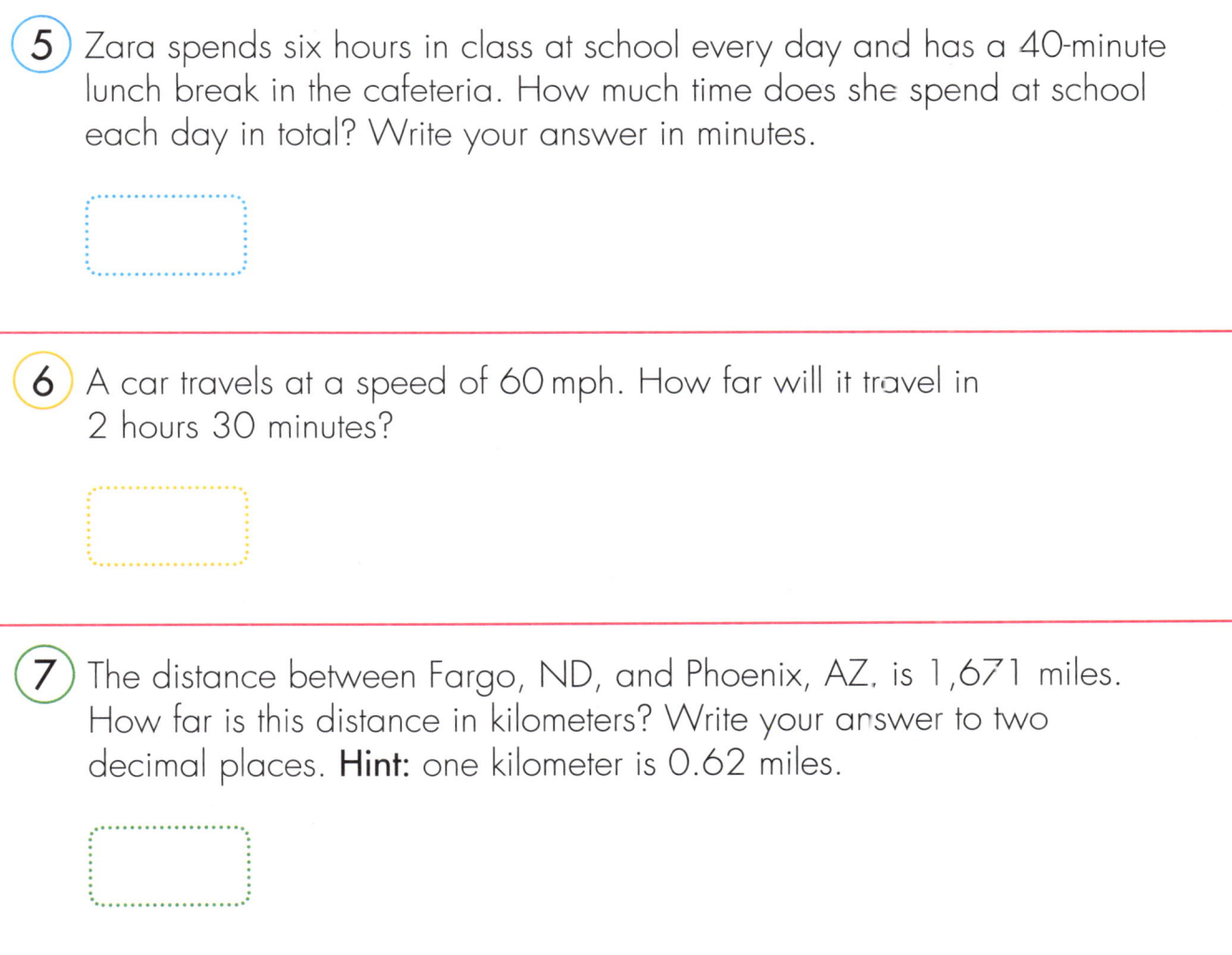

Harder Problems 1

These questions test many areas of math. Give them a try!

① Find the lowest number that has these factors: 1, 2, 3, 4, 6, and 12.

② What are the two prime numbers between 60 and 70?

☐ and ☐

③ The cost of a magazine was $6. During a sale, the cost was reduced by one-fourth. How much did the magazine cost during the sale?

④ The average cost of farmland is $3,700 per acre and a farmer plans to buy 12.5 acres of land. How much will the farmer have to pay for the land?

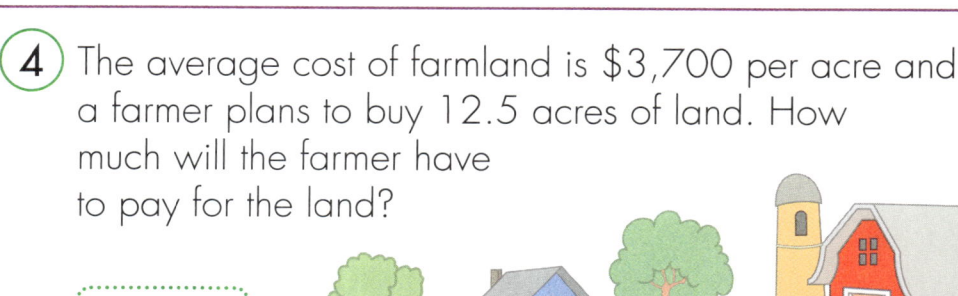

Time Filler:
Which prime numbers between zero and 20 have a square number and a multiple of three before and after them?

5) Anna's aunt moved from Birmingham, AL, to Winchester, VA. She sold her house in Birmingham for $364,890 and bought a house in Winchester for $521,000. What is the difference between the prices of the two houses?

6) The cost of driving an average car was $6,100 last year. If this amount rises 25% this year, what will be the new cost?

7) A number is squared and then doubled. The result is 72. What was the original number?

8) The average of two numbers is 18. If one of the numbers is 12, what is the other number?

Harder Problems 2

By now, you should be much more confident about tackling tricky problems. Try these!

1) Ann did her monthly grocery shopping in a local store and the bill was $600. The following month, she shopped in a new store and paid 25% less. How much did Ann pay in the new store?

2) 22,000 people were entitled to vote in a local election, but only 5,500 voted on election day. What fraction of people voted in the election?

3) Elsa scored 45 out of 50 on a math test. Anna scored 5 points less than Elsa. What fraction of the questions did Anna get right?

4) A workman earns $13.65 per hour on week days and twice this amount on Saturday. If he worked eight hours a day from Monday to Saturday, how much did he earn at the end of six days?

Time Filler:
If the area of a rectangle is 162 cm², what might be the lengths of the sides? Write as many possible combinations as you can.

5) In a class of 32 children, one-eighth had blond hair and the rest had brown hair. How many children had brown hair?

☐ children

6) The thickness of the metal used to make cars is 0.89 mm. In trucks, it is 2.10 mm. What is the difference in thickness of the metal used in cars and trucks?

☐

7) Nina multiplied 5 by the number of sides of an octagon. She divided the product by the number of sides of a hexagon. What answer did Nina arrive at? Show your answer in numbers and fractions.

☐

8) Arthur thought of a number and squared it. He multiplied the square by 10 and finally divided the product by three. The answer he arrived at was 480. What number did Arthur start with?

☐

Answers:

04–05 Fractions and Decimals 1
06–07 Fractions and Decimals 2

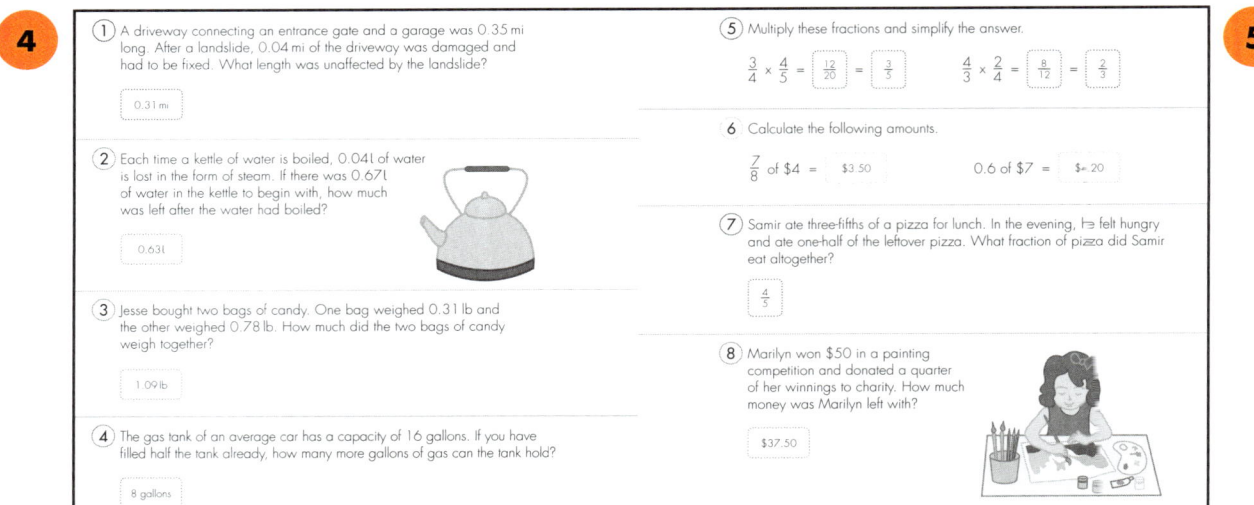

By now, your child should be able to solve simple fraction and decimal equations with ease. Keeping in mind the relationship between fractions and decimals will help him or her attempt problems with confidence.

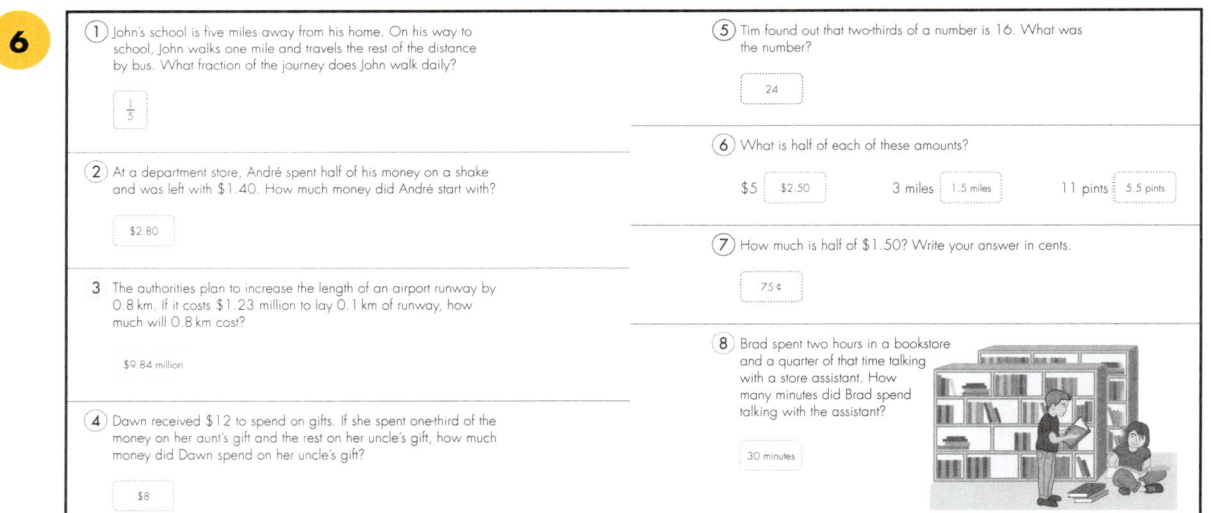

Your child should learn to convert instantly between fractions with fifths and tenths and their decimal equivalents. It is also useful to have a good knowledge of "awkward" fractions, such as $\frac{1}{3}$ and $\frac{1}{8}$.

Answers:

08–09 Fractions, Decimals, and Percentages 1
10–11 Fractions, Decimals, and Percentages 2

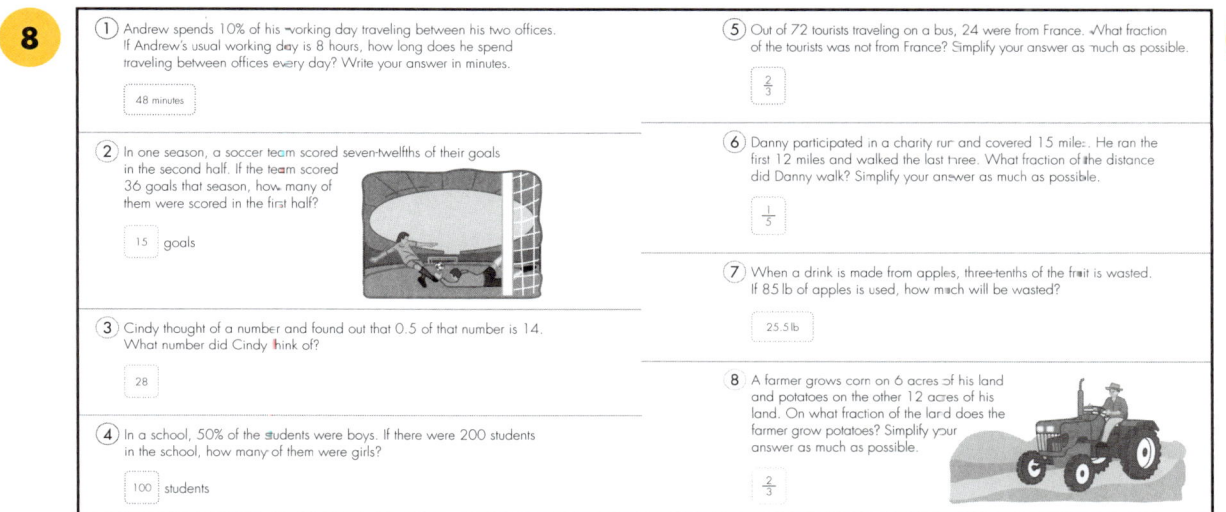

It is very important that your child be aware of the connection between fractions, decimals, and percentages. He or she will then understand how to convert one to the other, and will be able to convert the commonly used ones effortlessly.

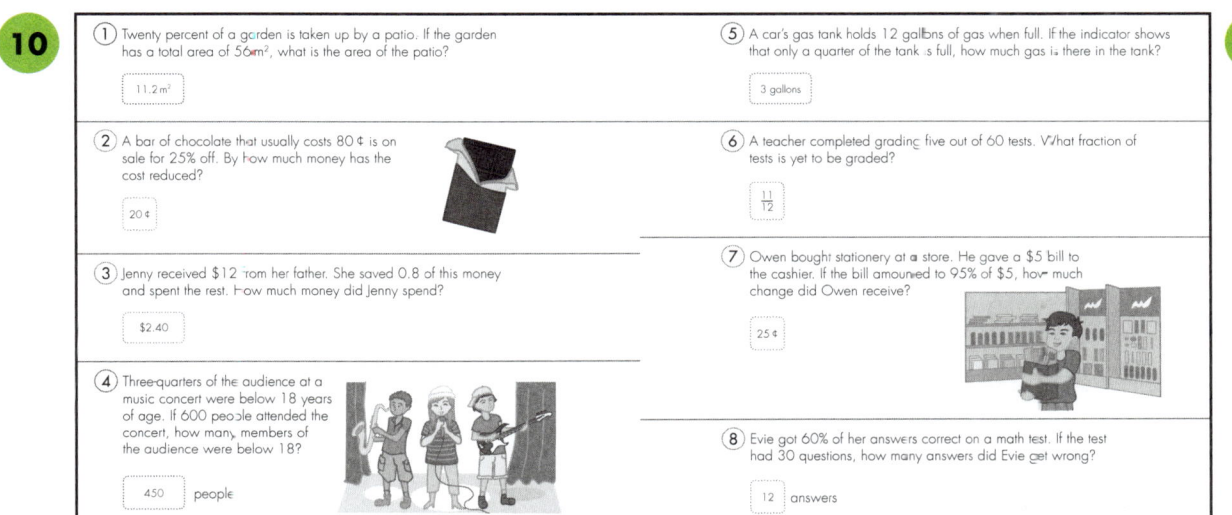

Once your child is able to clearly understand that 1¢ is 1% of $1 and 1 cm is 1% of 1 m, he or she will find it easy to calculate percentages of amounts—for example, 18% of $2.

Answers:

12–13 Percentage Problems 1
14–15 Percentage Problems 2

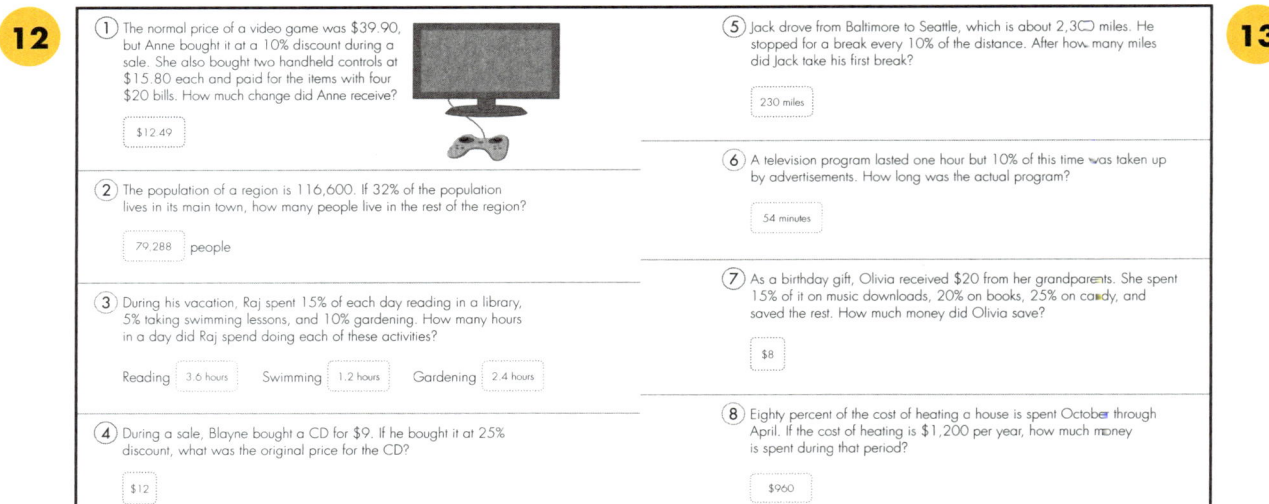

Each time your child has solved a problem, remind him or her to double-check the answer. A useful way to check a problem is to reverse the calculation, starting with the answer you have found and working back to the amounts given in the original equation.

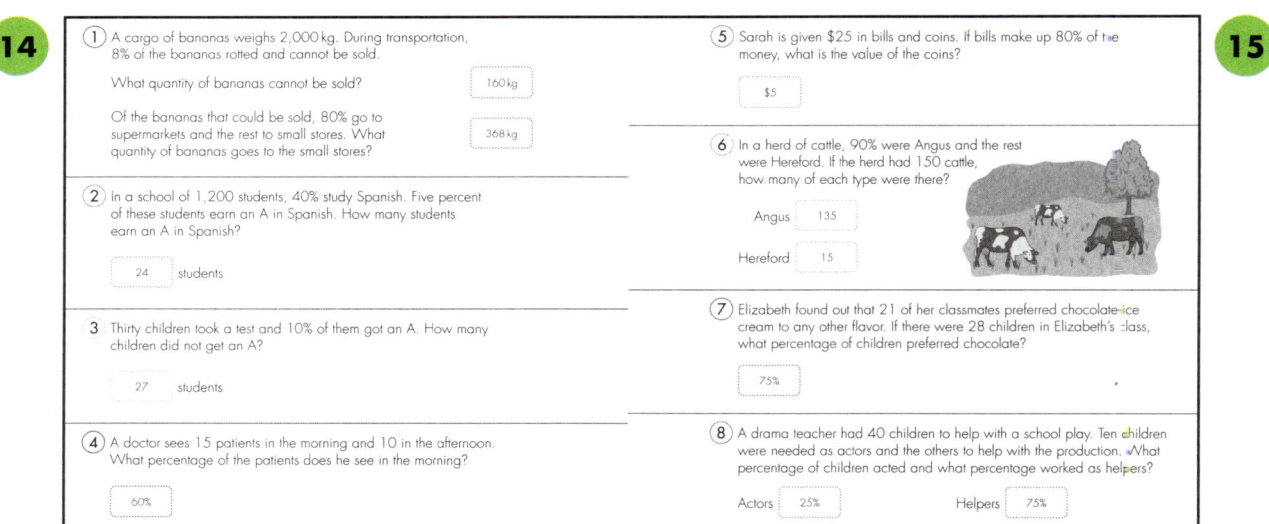

The more familiar your child is with the use of percentages in daily life, the more confident he or she will be when solving percentage problems.

Encourage your child to look out for percentage amounts in advertisements for banks, loans, and store sales.

Answers:

16-17 General Calculations 1

18-19 General Calculations 2

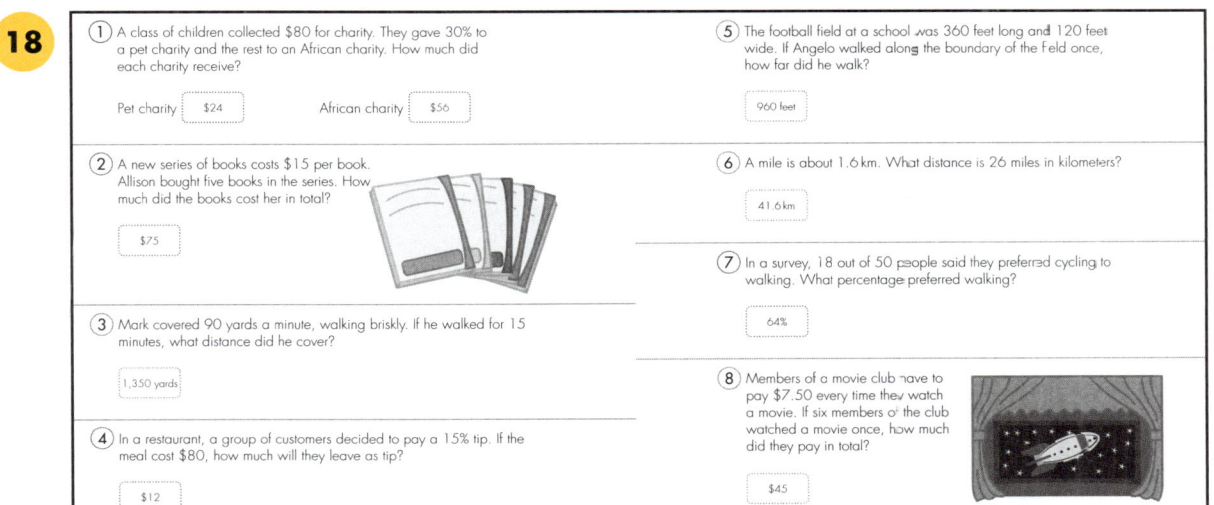

16

1. Emelia's dad gave her 5¢ on Sunday, double that amount on Monday, double that amount on Tuesday, and so on until Saturday.

   How much money did Emelia receive on Saturday? **$3.20**

   What was the total amount Emelia received from Sunday to Saturday? **$6.35**

2. Sean gave twice as much money to the Rescue a Rhino charity as he did to the Help a Hippo charity. If Sean gave $25 to Help a Hippo, how much money did he give to Rescue a Rhino? **$50**

3. A small township spends 20% of its money on education. If the township spends a total of one million dollars every year, how much money does it spend on education? **$200,000**

4. How many millimeters are the same as 2.45 m? **2,450 mm**

17

5. Beth needs to stock up on food for a six-day camping trip. If Beth spends $12 on each day's food, how much money will she spend in total? **$72**

6. Twelve out of every 1,000 dollar bills are damaged. What percentage of dollar bills is this? **1.2%**

7. Jimmy normally receives $12 as allowance each week. The week before Christmas, he is given an extra 25%. How much will Jimmy be given in total that week? **$15**

8. Mary has to divide a piece of material, which is 12 yards long, into six-inch strips. How many strips of equal length will Mary make? **72** strips

As a tip for working out general problems, it is useful to read each question once and then read it a second time, carefully underlining and highlighting the most important aspects of the problem. Encourage your child to adopt this approach if he or she is having trouble.

18

1. A class of children collected $80 for charity. They gave 30% to a pet charity and the rest to an African charity. How much did each charity receive?

   Pet charity **$24** African charity **$56**

2. A new series of books costs $15 per book. Allison bought five books in the series. How much did the books cost her in total? **$75**

3. Mark covered 90 yards a minute, walking briskly. If he walked for 15 minutes, what distance did he cover? **1,350 yards**

4. In a restaurant, a group of customers decided to pay a 15% tip. If the meal cost $80, how much will they leave as tip? **$12**

19

5. The football field at a school was 360 feet long and 120 feet wide. If Angelo walked along the boundary of the field once, how far did he walk? **960 feet**

6. A mile is about 1.6 km. What distance is 26 miles in kilometers? **41.6 km**

7. In a survey, 18 out of 50 people said they preferred cycling to walking. What percentage preferred walking? **64%**

8. Members of a movie club have to pay $7.50 every time they watch a movie. If six members of the club watched a movie once, how much did they pay in total? **$45**

When working on math problems, your child should show his or her work clearly and logically. Poorly written figures that are jumbled together will not help your child reach the solution quickly. They will slow him or her down.

Answers:

20–21 General Calculations 3
22–23 Conversion Problems 1, see p.80
24–25 Addition and Subtraction 1

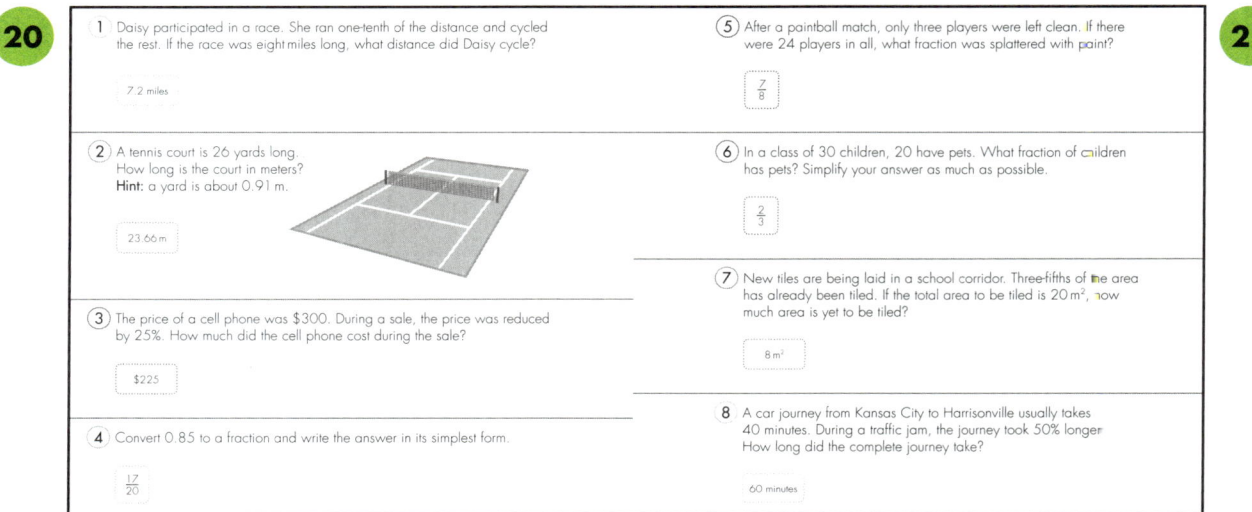

Some children find working to a time limit a fun challenge, while others find it stressful. Remind your child to relax, carefully read each question, and do his or her best.

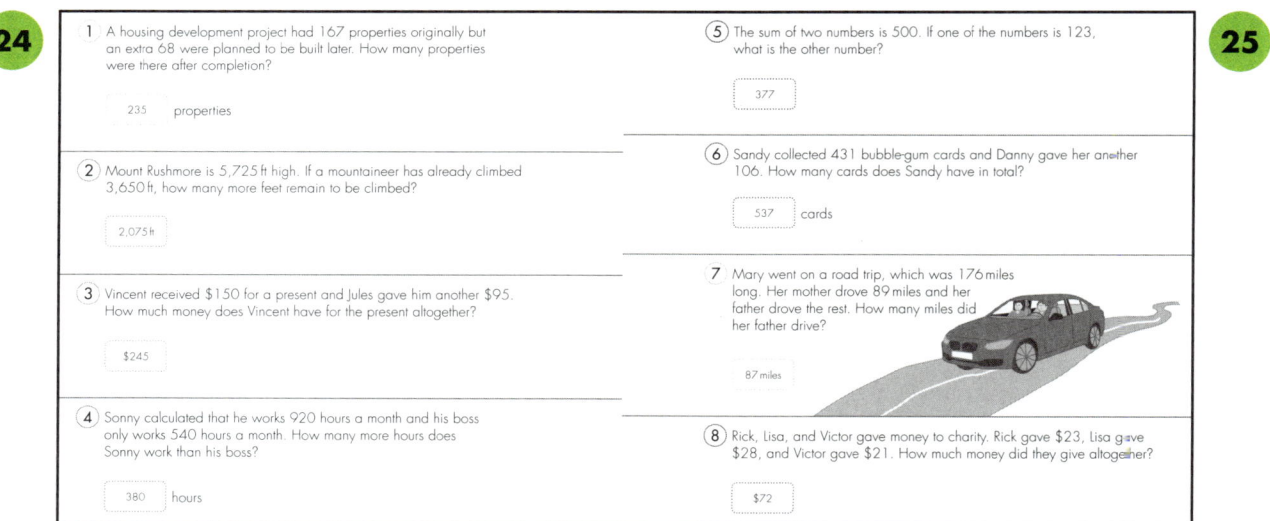

Encourage your child to imagine the problem as a real situation as this may help him or her to visualize the calculations that need to be carried out.

Answers:

26–27 Addition and Subtraction 2
28–29 Fractions, Decimals, and Percentages 3

26

1. Out of 496 peaches at a fruit mart, 164 were rotten and could not be sold. How many peaches could be sold?
   332 peaches

2. A small town had a population of 1,168 people. 1,096 people left the town after a drought. What was the population after the people left?
   72 people

3. When 250 is added to a number, the answer is 800. What was the original number?
   550

4. A number is twice the value of another number. If the two numbers are added together, the total is 36. What are the two numbers?
   12 and **24**

27

5. Will decreased a number by 58 and the new number was 76. What number did Will start with?
   134

6. A town had 677 streetlights. As part of a development project, 42 new lights were put up. How many streetlights are there in total?
   719 streetlights

7. The total of three numbers is 1,000. If two of the numbers are 180 and 360, what is the third number?
   460

8. Amy goes for a picnic to the countryside with her parents. The total distance is 68 miles. If they have already covered 43 miles, how much more distance do they still need to travel?
   25 miles

If time allows, ask your child to make some rough calculations in his or her head and write down an estimation for his or her answers. Then have your child compare the estimates with the actual answers.

28

1. Write each fraction as a decimal.

   $\frac{9}{10}$ **0.9** $\frac{7}{100}$ **0.07** $\frac{2}{10}$ **0.2**

   $\frac{1}{10}$ **0.1** $\frac{4}{10}$ **0.4** $\frac{4}{100}$ **0.04**

   $\frac{5}{10}$ **0.5** $\frac{11}{100}$ **0.11** $\frac{21}{100}$ **0.21**

2. The cost of building a house is twice the cost of the land it is built on. If building a house costs $250,000, how much has the land cost?
   $125,000

3. In a factory with 72 workers, one-sixth of the workers are male. How many workers are female?
   60 workers

4. Orange squash is a drink that is made by mixing one part concentrate to four parts water. At a party, four pints of concentrate are used. How many pints of water will be needed?
   16 pints

29

5. What fraction of letters in the English alphabet are vowels? (Assume that the letter y is a consonant.)
   $\frac{5}{26}$

6. In a parking lot with 100 spaces, 35% of the spaces are reserved. How many spaces are open?
   65 parking spaces

7. In a box of chocolates, one-fourth of the candy was dark chocolate and the rest was milk chocolate. If there were 36 milk chocolates, how many dark chocolates were there?
   12 dark chocolates

8. Every time Ben plants three daisies, Pam plants one rose. If Pam planted 100 roses, how many daisies did Ben plant?
   300 daisies

Help your child understand that using fractions, decimals, and percentages are different ways of expressing parts of a whole. Encourage him or her to read these questions very carefully before solving.

Answers:

30–31 Fractions and Decimals 3
32–33 Area Problems 1

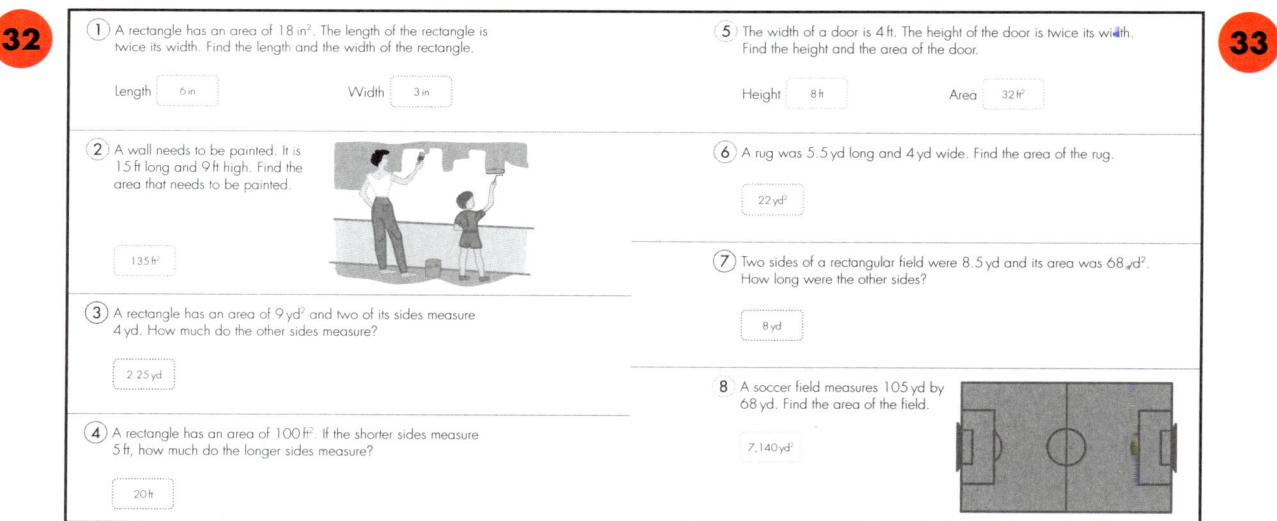

When your child is solving these problems, ensure that he or she always checks that a result is sensible. As these are practical problems, a slight mistake in calculation may result in an answer he or she can immediately identify as incorrect or impossible.

Your child may find it easy to work out area problems. However, it is good to remind him or her to write the units at the end of the answers.

Answers will be incomplete without units. Most units can be written in more than one way—for example, "square inches" or "in²."

Answers:

34–35 Area Problems 2
36–37 Multiplication and Division 1

34

1) A sidewalk measures 30 yd by 3 yd. What is its area?
   90 yd²

2) A picture frame is a square with each side measuring 13 in. What is the area of the frame?
   169 in²

3) The area of a table top is 15 ft². What is half the area of the table top?
   7.5 ft²

4) A square has an area of 225 in². What is the length of each side of the square?
   15 in

35

5) The screen of a TV installed outside a fast-food joint is 56 in wide and 30 in high. What is the area of the screen?
   1,680 in²

6) The height of a greeting card is twice its length. If the area of the card is 18 in², what are the lengths of the sides?
   3 in and **6 in**

7) A laptop has a screen, which is 13 in wide and 9 in high. What is the area of the screen?
   117 in²

8) If a wall tile has an area of 24 in², what will be the area of 6 such tiles?
   144 in²

It is useful for your child to calculate the areas of some rectangular and square objects at home. It will help your child apply the formulas he or she is learning at school.

36

1) Every time Larry caught a frog in a computer game, he gained 15 points. If Larry catches 20 frogs, how many points will he have?
   300 points

2) Alex scored three times as many points as the boy seated next to him on a math test. If the boy scored 35 points, how many points did Alex score?
   105 points

3) Lucy distributed 30 cookies equally among five of her friends. How many cookies did each friend receive?
   6 cookies

4) When Clark played a computer game, he gained 50 points every time he caught a bad guy. Clark had a good day and caught 12 bad guys. How many points did he score that day?
   600 points

37

5) The length of a rectangle is 1.5 cm and the width is 8 cm. Find its area.
   12 cm²

6) Perry's birthday cake was cut into eight pieces and each piece had six chocolate candies on top. How many chocolate candies were there in total on the cake?
   48 chocolate candies

7) Jimmy's parents give him allowance of 50¢ every week. If Jimmy has saved his money for 20 weeks to go on a vacation, how much money has he collected? Give your answer in dollars.
   $10

8) A teacher graded 30 tests each evening for five evenings. How many tests did the teacher grade in total?
   150 tests

Before beginning this type of exercise, have your child "warm up" by him or her going through some of the higher times tables, such as 20, 25, and 50.

Answers:

38–39 Multiplication and Division 2
40–41 General Calculations 4

38
1. George multiplied a number by itself and got the answer 81. What number did George begin with?
   9
2. A driver collects five coupons every time he gets his gas tank refilled. If the driver refills 35 times in a year, how many coupons will he collect?
   175 coupons
3. Billy divides a number by six and the result is 5 remainder 3. What number did Billy begin with?
   33
4. A mailman delivers to 28 streets. Each street has 20 houses. How many houses does the mailman deliver to?
   560 houses

39
5. A math teacher wrote 20 equations on the board and in the evening she checked the students' answers. If the teacher had to check 240 answers, how many children are in her class?
   12 children
6. Billy pays $15 every time he takes a swimming lesson. If Billy takes twelve lessons, how much will they cost him?
   $180
7. A number multiplied by nine gives 180. What is the number?
   20
8. When a number is divided by five, the answer is 12 remainder 3. What is the number?
   63

Have your child ask you some multiplication and division questions. Answer the questions, then ask your child to tell you if your answers are correct. This is a fun way for your child to exercise his or her skills.

40
1. Stefan's father has to pay $114 for a train ticket to New York, but his grandfather pays 60% of that amount. How much less money does Stefan's father have to pay?
   $45.60
2. A waiter has calculated a customer's bill as $56. He then realizes he has added an extra meal and needs to reduce the bill by 25%. How much will the new bill be after the reduction?
   $42
3. When three different numbers are added together, their total is 47. One of the numbers is 20 and one of the other numbers is half the third number. What are the other two numbers?
   9 and **18**
4. If half of an amount is $26, what is the full amount?
   $52

41
5. When a number is multiplied by 12 and then halved, the result is 120. What is the original number?
   20
6. Which three consecutive numbers add up to give a total of 90?
   Hint: consecutive numbers are numbers that follow each other in order.
   29 **30** **31**
7. If the time now is 11:00 AM, what time will it be two hours later?
   1:00 PM
8. If it costs $150 to heat a house each month, how much will it cost for a whole year?
   $1,800

Explain to your child that it is vital to read the question carefully before attempting to solve it. A question may have a "trick" ending, so very careful reading will help your child identify it.

Answers:

42–43 General Calculations 5
44–45 General Calculations 6

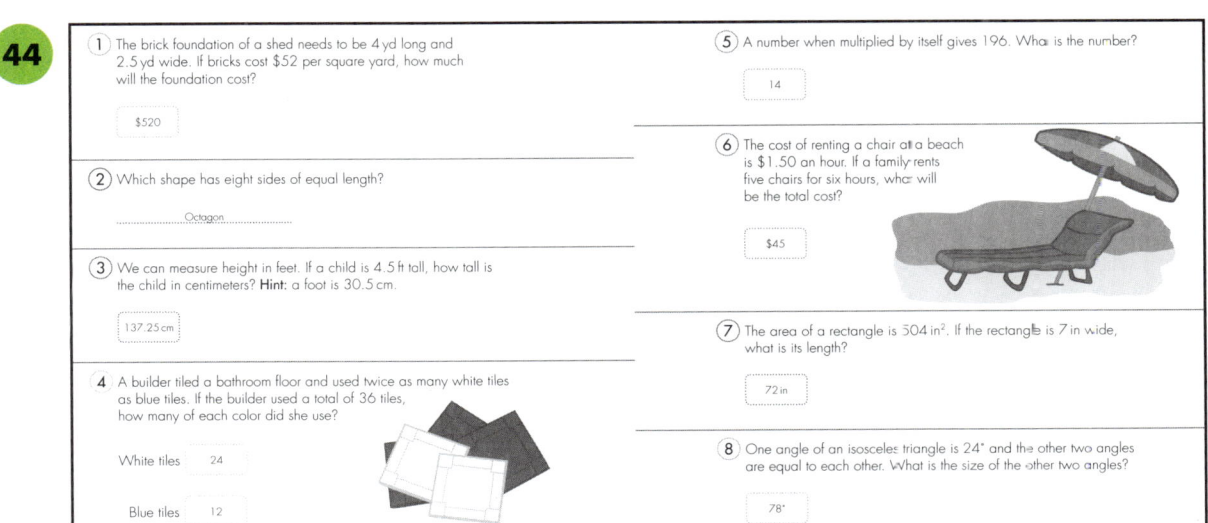

When your child is attempting complicated problems, he or she should decide on a plan or order in which to approach the solution. This approach becomes increasingly important as your child moves toward intermediate or middle school.

Your child is likely to be very familiar with times tables at this point in his or her studies. To help him or her solve these problems confidently, make sure your child can quickly work out the factors of numbers at least to 100.

Answers:

46–47 Conversion Problems 2, see p.80
48–49 Understanding Charts 1
50–51 Understanding Charts 2

48–49

Thirty children were asked to describe how they felt about school examinations. This pie chart shows their views.

Children's Views on School Examinations

5, 3, 10, 12
- Enjoyed
- Didn't like
- Anxious
- Didn't mind

1) What fraction of the children didn't mind taking exams? — $\frac{1}{6}$

2) Which was the largest group? — Anxious

3) What percentage of the children enjoyed exams? — 10%

4) How many more children didn't like exams than the ones who enjoyed them? — 7 children

5) What fraction of the total number of children were either anxious or didn't like the exams? — $\frac{11}{15}$

6) Which group was two less than those who were anxious? — Didn't like

7) What was the average number of votes for each response? — 7.5 votes

8) If six children had said that they didn't mind taking exams, what fraction of the children would that be? — $\frac{1}{5}$

In our daily lives, we are surrounded by displays that represent all sorts of information. Encourage your child to look carefully at such displays. Ask questions that will test his or her ability to interpret them.

50–51

A teacher made a note of the number of children who ate fruit at lunchtime. These are her findings.

Day	Number of Children
Monday	15
Tuesday	26
Wednesday	20
Thursday	18
Friday	16

1) What is the average amount of fruit eaten each day? — 19

2) How many more children ate fruit on Tuesday than on Monday? — 11 children

3) What fraction of the total amount of fruit was eaten on Monday? — $\frac{3}{19}$

4) Which day has the median number of fruit? — Thursday
Hint: median is the middle value in a series of numbers.

During the next week, each child was given free fruit every day and the teacher prepared a new chart.

Day	Number of Children This Week	Number of Children Last Week
Monday	36	15
Tuesday	51	26
Wednesday	40	20
Thursday	46	18
Friday	45	16

5) Which day had the largest increase in the number of children eating fruit? — Friday

6) Which day has the median number of fruit this week? — Friday

7) Which day has the smallest increase in the number of children eating fruit? — Wednesday

8) What is the average amount of fruit eaten each day this week? — 43.5

It can be fun to sit with your child and make line graphs, bar charts, and even pie charts using a simple computer program. Always remember to label them clearly; in school, graphs and charts without clear labels will often be marked incomplete.

Answers:

52–53 Time Problems

54–55 Simple Formulas 1

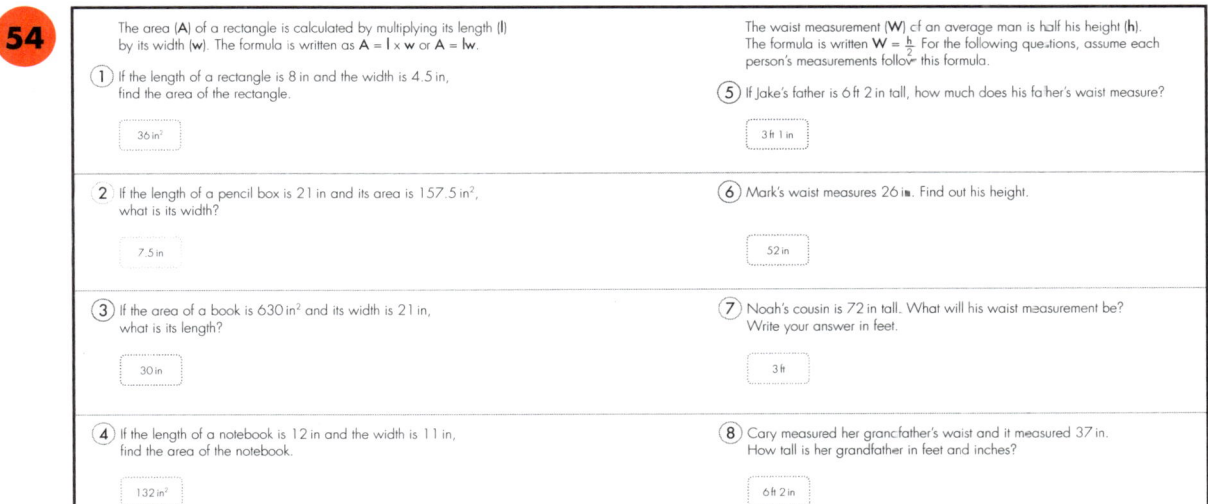

When appropriate, ask your child what time it will be after 10 minutes or what time it was 10 minutes ago. Vary the number of minutes as their confidence in time problems grows.

The introduction of simple formulas is new to the curriculum for this age, so your child may not have covered it at school yet. They are fairly straightforward, so try to help him or her initially with simple examples.

Answers:

56–57 Simple Formulas 2
58–59 General Calculations 7

56

1. $a = b + c$ means a is the sum of b and c.

   If a is 19 and c is 7, find the value of b. **12**

   If c is 18 and a is 42, find the value of b. **24**

   If b is 29 and a is 58, find the value of c. **29**

2. $a = b \times c$ means a is the product of b multiplied by c.

   If b is 3.5 and c is 8, find the value of a. **28**

   If a is 70 and b is 14, find the value of c. **5**

   If a is 12, give three different pairs of whole numbers that could be the values of b and c.

   1 and 12   **3 and 4**   **2 and 6**

57

3. If $a = b - c$ and a is 10, write three different pairs of numbers that b and c could be. Answers may vary.

   11 – 1   **12 – 2**   **13 – 3**

4. If $a = \frac{b}{c}$ and the value of a is 4, write three pairs of numbers that could be the values of b and c. Answers may vary.

   4 and 1   **8 and 2**   **12 and 3**

5. If $a = 3b$ and b is 4, what is a? **Hint:** $3b$ means $3 \times b$. **12**

6. If $a = 3b$ and a is 21, what is b? **7**

7. If $a = 2b + 4$ and the value of a is 16, what is b? **6**

8. $a = 2b + 4$ means a is equal to twice b plus 4. If b is 6, what is a? **16**

Your child needs to learn the formulas that are used to find the areas of simple shapes, including squares, rectangles, parallelograms, and triangles.

58

1. A packet contains six greetings cards and costs $4.68. What is the average cost of each card? **78¢**

2. Dan added three consecutive numbers and his total came to 45. Which numbers did he add? **14 15 16**

3. Add the number of sides of an octagon to the number of sides of a decagon. Then divide the total by the number of sides of a triangle and write the answer. **6**

4. Jake and his dad covered a total distance of 130 miles in 2 hours. At what speed did his dad drive the car? **65 mph**

59

5. What amount is halfway between $70 and $100? **$85**

6. Martin spends $55 a month on food and Danny spends twice as much. How much money does Danny spend? **$110**

7. If a square has an area of 144 in², what is the length of each side? **12 in**

8. On an average, a cow gives 1,600 gallons of milk each year. If a herd has 60 cows, how much milk will the herd give in one year? **96,000 gallons**

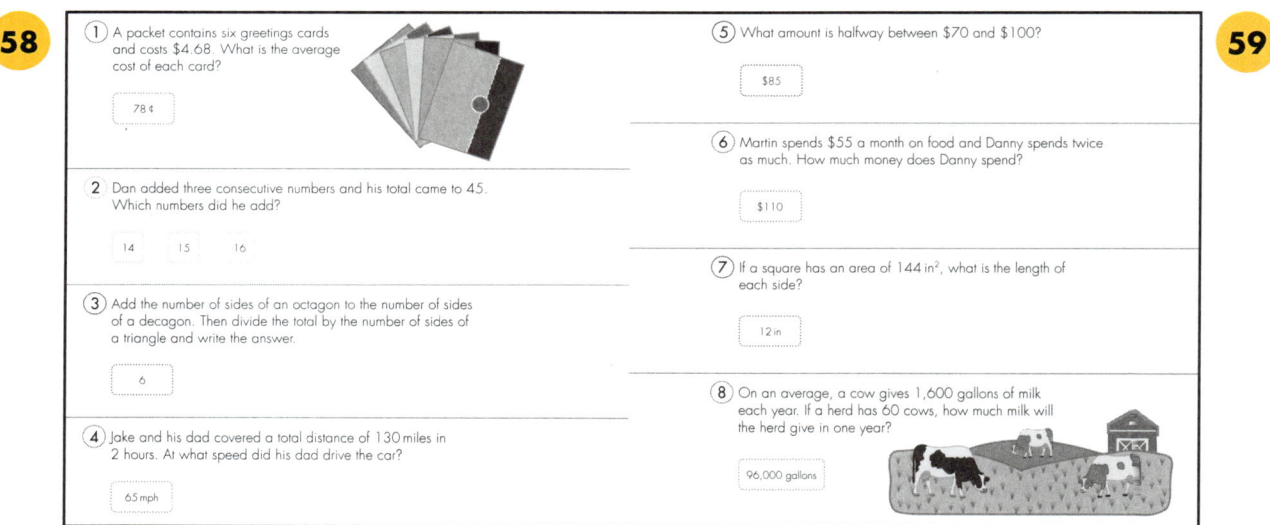

Before starting on these problems, ask your child how he or she plans to get started, and what methods he or she will use and why. Your child may find it useful to discuss his or her reasoning with you.

Answers:

60–61 Conversion Problems 3, see p.80
62–63 Harder Problems 1
64–65 Harder Problems 2

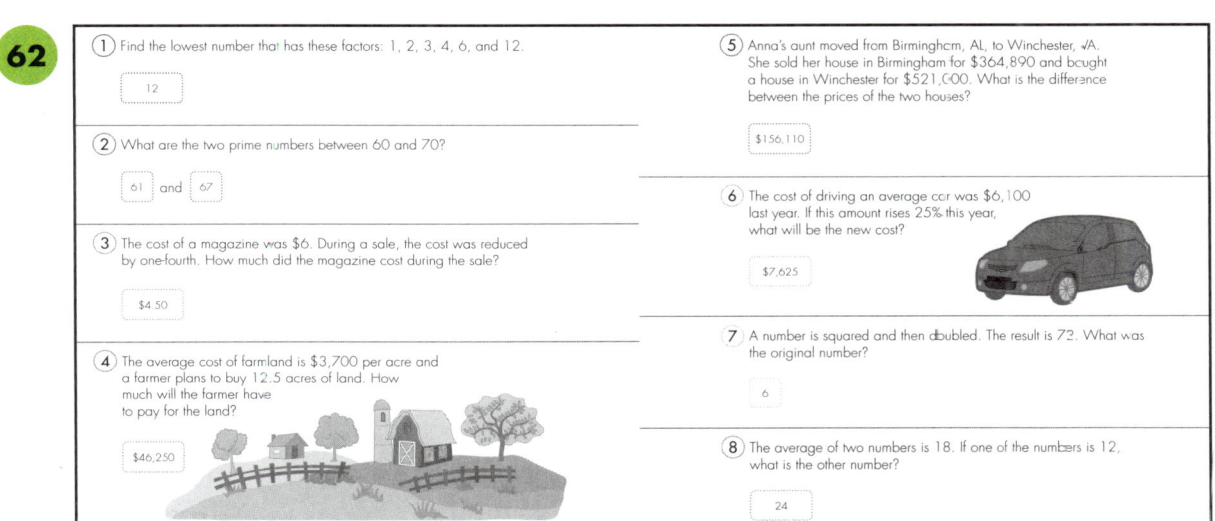

If possible, get your child to answer each question without using paper and pencil. Encourage him or her to work out the problems in his or her head as far as possible.

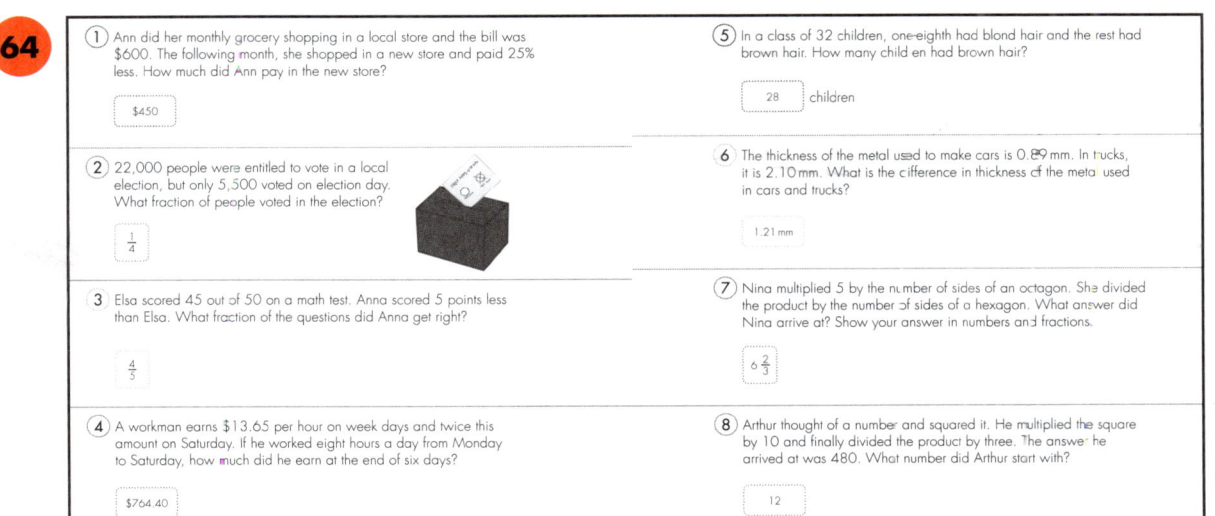

Make sure your child follows these steps while attempting tricky problems: read the question very carefully, underline or mark important information if necessary, estimate the answer if appropriate, write the calculation clearly, calculate correctly, and check if the answer is reasonable.

Answers:

22–23 Conversion Problems 1
46–47 Conversion Problems 2
60–61 Conversion Problems 3

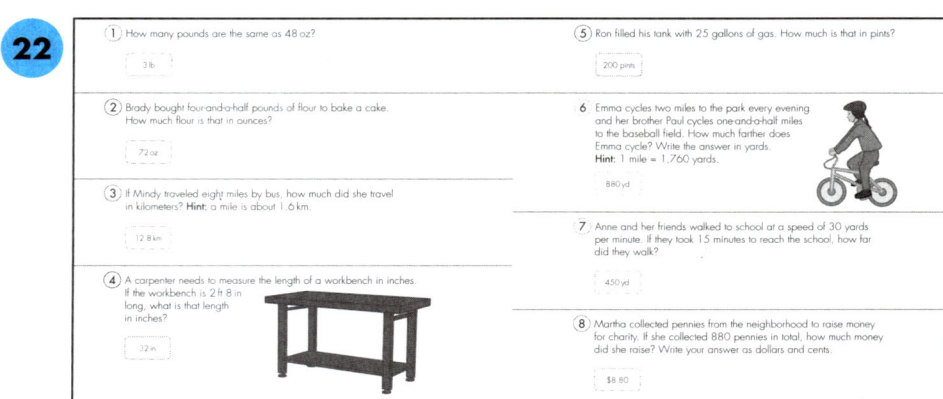

Many children are confident with well-known units and conversions, such as centimeters to meters. However, they are often less sure about smaller or larger units, such as millimeters and kilometers. The more experience they have with conversions, the easier these problems will be.

Your child should know the "half" and "quarter" of amounts—for example, half and quarter of inches, feet, yards, pints, and gallons.

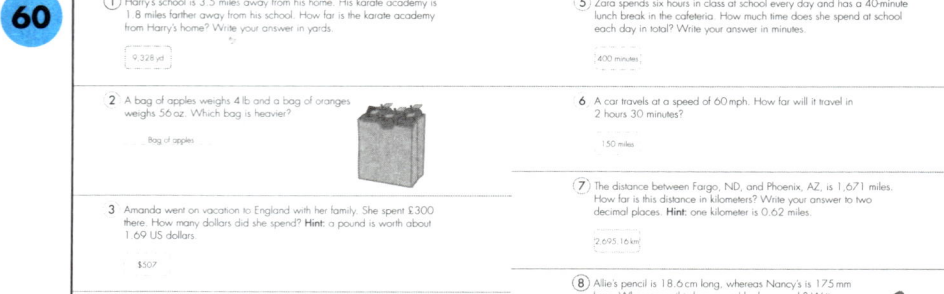

If your child is not familiar with the concept of international currencies, question 3 on this page may prove difficult. Talk to your child about currencies such as pounds, euros, and yen so he or she is well informed.